AUNTIE VIE

Auntie Vie surrounded by photos of her family.
ROLF HICKER PHOTOGRAPHY

A Life
of Pickles
and Pearls

Auntie Vie

as told to Cathy Converse

TouchWood
Editions

TouchWood Editions
www.touchwoodeditions.com

Canadian Cataloguing in Publication information
is available from Library and Archives Canada

Editor: Marlyn Horsdal
Cover image: Rolf Hicker Photography
Interior images: All photos not otherwise credited were taken by the author.
Design and illustrations: Pete Kohut

BRITISH COLUMBIA
ARTS COUNCIL
Supported by the Province of British Columbia

Canada Council   Conseil des Arts
for the Arts   du Canada

We gratefully acknowledge the financial support for our publishing activities
from the Government of Canada through the Canada Book Fund, Canada
Council for the Arts, and the province of British Columbia through the
British Columbia Arts Council and the Book Publishing Tax Credit.

Mixed Sources
Cert no. SW-COC-001271
© 1996 FSC

FSC

This book was produced using FSC-certified, acid free paper,
processed chlorine free and printed with vegetable-based inks.

The recipes in this book have been tested for accuracy and the information in
this book is true and complete to the best of our knowledge. The author and
publisher disclaim any liability in connection with the use of this information.

1 2 3 4 5 13 12 11 10

PRINTED IN CANADA

To Christina.
When it is your turn to take up the mantle as
matriarch of the family, remember to keep a
spring in your step and a smile in your heart.

Age is an issue of mind over matter.
If you don't mind, it doesn't matter.
—Mark Twain

contents

Preface

AUNTIE VIE SPARKLES ON TELEVISION

We first met her while watching *Dancing with the Stars* during the spring of 2010. A record twenty-four million of us tuned in to watch celebrities compete for a mirror-ball trophy. When the debut episode was over, the person who had made the most impact was not a star—it was Pamela Anderson's eighty-five-year-old great-aunt, Vie.

Perhaps it was her dynamic outfit. Perhaps it was her infectious laugh. Perhaps we felt it was sweet that Anderson would compete in a televised dance competition because Vie was a fan of the show. No matter the reason for our initial interest in Auntie Vie; it quickly became clear she was a star in her own right.

A team from Vancouver Island's */A\ News* visited Vie the next day in her home. During the interview, we learned about her award-winning pickle recipe and her impressive shoe collection. Off camera, she was a gracious hostess, serving the reporter and cameraman slices of her homemade pie.

The local television audience reacted to the interview with adoring e-mails and word-of-mouth praise. Everybody loved Vie and wanted to see more. */A\ News* responded by visiting Vie weekly. While her primary role

Adam Sawatsky from /A\ *News* interviewing Auntie Vie as she was judging a cook-off between the Fairmont Empress and the Inn at Laurel Point in Victoria.

was to comment on her great-niece's dancing, the most compelling moments of the coverage were getting to know the woman behind the larger-than-life personality.

Auntie Vie embodies glamour yet remains down to earth. She oozes creativity and positivity. Her work ethic is prodigious. Her capacity for caring is enormous, enveloping family and rescued pets.

While millions were tuning in to see Anderson tackle the cha-cha and the tango, Auntie Vie was earning a formidable audience of her own. The local coverage on Vie was followed by interviews on syndicated US radio and television shows. She appeared regularly on Canada's most-watched national entertainment show, *eTalk*, and America's number one celebrity show, *Access Hollywood*. Both programs flew crews to Vancouver Island for interviews. A Google search for Auntie Vie turned up more than twenty-nine thousand hits.

Vie is responding to the international attention with aplomb. She says she is grateful to be recognized after so many years of being retired and pleased to have the opportunity to "cheer people up."

Perhaps it is we who are most thankful that we have been given the chance to get to know Auntie Vie—a woman who sparkles both inside and out.

—Adam Sawatsky
Entertainment Anchor/Reporter
/A\ Vancouver Island

Introduction

Auntie Vie is the matriarch of her large, extended family, and the fairy godmother of spunk, sass, fun, fashion, and cooking; she's the guru of aging with joy. She has been compared to Auntie Mame by some of her fans. Auntie Vie first came to media attention in February 2010 with the publication of a newspaper article in Victoria, British Columbia, where she lives. The piece focused on a stunning hat Auntie Vie had received as a gift from her great-niece, Pamela Anderson. The hat was designed by London milliner extraordinaire Philip Treacy and was evidently chosen for her by Philip Treacy himself. The hat is "fun, wild, cheerful and colorful for such a great lady," Pamela was reported as saying, and it is all of that. People from Vancouver Island knew about Pamela but had not met her great-aunt. Pamela hails from Ladysmith and islanders are familiar with her star personality as well as her good works.

The reporter went on to write about Auntie Vie's close relationship with her great-niece and Vie's roots: growing up barefoot in the heart of Saskatchewan and living on a hayrack. The juxtaposition of haute couture and bare feet was too hard to pass up and other newspapers quickly picked up the article. People began asking who this auntie was; she was shown in one photograph

with a funky, bejeweled, pink cowboy hat, which she had bought for Pamela's wedding to Kid Rock, and in another as a stylish elder stateswoman with *un chapeau élégant* gracing her head. There was a quiet buzz for a while.

Despite people's interest, the story might have stopped there, but toward the beginning of the following month, in March, Pamela debuted as one of the celebrity stars in ABC's reality television program *Dancing with the Stars*. Vancouver Island was watching, as were nearly twenty-four million others across North America. In her dedication, Pamela very quietly said that she was dancing for her mother and for her Auntie Vie. She knew how much her great-aunt enjoyed dancing, for Vie had been two-stepping and waltzing since she was three years old. The thing is, Auntie Vie is an octogenarian; she is eighty-five years old. The media were intrigued. By the end of the month, Auntie Vie had been on *The Billy Bush Show*, CBS *News*, *eTalk*, and the *Wendy Williams Show*, and featured in USA *Today*, *Vulture*—the online entertainment section of *New York Magazine*—the Saskatoon *Star Phoenix*, and the *Ottawa Citizen*, to name but a few.

Vie's memory is sharp and she kept the names of the producers, shows and interviewers straight except for one occasion. There was a charming incident when she was in a live telephone conversation with Billy Bush during his television program on *Access Hollywood*. When he introduced himself, Auntie Vie asked him to repeat his name; it was her fourth interview that day. He seemed a bit taken aback and responded by saying, "I'm actually quite famous." Her comment was, "That's nice, dear." That's Auntie Vie.

There was more to come. The media wanted to do cooking shows with her; they clamored after her comments on fashion; she was asked to judge dancing contests and act as a celebrity chef commenting on cooking contests between well-known hotels. People were eager for her thoughts on aging and on life. She sat in front of a computer screen at four o'clock in the morning to do live television interviews; she became a master of retakes; she settled quite easily into walking around with a small black microphone hooked onto the back of her clothing; and she learned the word "bling" to describe her jewelry. There have been tweets, Facebook entries and blogs about her. Vulture tweeted, "We talked to the woman who warmed our hearts on *Dancing with the Stars.*" Another commented, "We now know where Pam gets her drop-dead gorgeous looks from." An anonymous tweeter stated, "The world needs more Auntie Vies," and Wendy Williams blogged, "Love Auntie Vie. Someone that age to be so alert is a blessing . . ."

Vie became an overnight sensation. The media and the public couldn't get enough of her. It might have been too much for an elderly woman with a heart condition, but this was Auntie Vie. She was coached through the media blitz with help from Adam Sawatsky, Vancouver Island's /A\ *News* Entertainment Anchor, who interviewed her every Tuesday following Pamela's performances on Monday night's *Dancing with the Stars.* Adam knew what a jewel of a person Auntie Vie is and shared his enthusiasm with the rest of her fans. He showcased her fashion, her pies and pickles, her humor, and her bits of wisdom.

On Tuesday evenings Auntie Vie would have her neighbors over to watch the results of *Dancing with the Stars.* She was an enthusiastic supporter of her great-niece: she had many of her neighbors voting; she got people at the University of Victoria to vote; she even went into a neighborhood pub and told them to vote.

When Pamela was eliminated on the May 4 show, she said she would have to go into support mode for her two biggest fans, her mother and her Auntie Vie. She jokingly said, "No more block parties for my Auntie Vie."

Vie is very proud of her great-niece: "That little girl worked so hard. She had never danced before and she was practising eight hours a day. It all paid off. She was beautiful and graceful and got right into character. She danced her heart out. I couldn't be more proud."

Once again, Auntie Vie's celebrity could have vanished. We are, after all, in a time in which stars come and go with lightning speed as the media search for the next sound bite, but something unique happened between the public and Auntie Vie. There was an instant connection. We liked her and she genuinely liked us, and she was having fun. She has become a star in her own right, recognized wherever she goes. People talk about her at church groups, in auto shops, in beauty parlors—just drop the name "Auntie Vie" and the instant response is, "I love Auntie Vie!" The reasons for her popularity and staying power are simple. She represents so much of what we strive for in our lives: glamour, sparkle, fun, compassion, humility, wisdom, thoughtfulness, and complete comfort with her age and her life circumstances. She makes no apologies for who she is.

Perhaps Carol Anderson, her niece, best sums up Auntie Vie: "Auntie Vie finds good in everybody, even if it's not easily recognizable. She loves people, she listens, she is not judgmental, she is funny, she never complains, she has no guilt, she loves to dance, she is feminine, she is fashionable, she is witty, and she has taught us all that sixty or seventy is not the end—in Auntie Vie's case, not even close. For our family she fills the gap for those of us who have lost our parents. We just love her."

Vie's niece and great-niece, Carol Anderson and her daughter Pamela Anderson.

Perhaps that's what people sense in her. She shows us who we can be and she does it with love. Life is fragile and sometimes it can really hurt. We all need a little Auntie Vie in our lives.

Here's an introduction from Pamela Anderson:

I've been asked to write something about my Auntie Vie. Oh dear—I think she is a woman too hard to put into words. To meet her is to be captured by her style and love. She is a survivor amongst survivors— I wish my Grandma Rose were here to share this experience with her sister Vie. She would get a kick out of this. These are the most loving women I know, next to my mom; the sacrifice and grace all these woman share are a blessing to those around them. I'm fortunate—I'm sure I gained my real hard-work ethic from them—a selfless demeanor, I hope, and a glitz-and-glamour style to top it off, passed down through the generations.

Life is fun—it's a choice and it's a challenge. No one said it would be easy and as soon as we grasp that, we can accept our circumstances and enjoy things more. Everyone has a reason to complain but that's a lousy excuse. We say: share your love through cooking and turn a head—leave them wanting more. Do for everyone you can, despite any difficulty, despite the rules. All I can say is pickles, champagne and glitter! Being a woman is so much fun, and Auntie Vie is a classic example, an inspiration. When in doubt, when you don't know what else to do, just dance, sing, cook, make people laugh, and laugh at yourself. Be beautiful and charming—be a light in the world!

God bless,

Pamela

Auntie Vie has been a neighbor of mine for over fifteen years. We live quite close so I cannot help witnessing her comings and goings, and I count myself lucky to have her as my neighbor for she has always been gracious and charming. We nod as we take the garbage out in the evening—me in my loud Hawaiian print pajamas, T-shirt and Chaco sandals with Vibram soles and Auntie Vie in her long, flowing satin housecoat and slipper satin mules with beautiful pompoms. The difference is not lost on me. I need to smarten up my look, I tell myself. She has a delightful sense of style and flair, and she has had me running outside many times with my point-and-shoot to take yet another picture of a beautiful outfit as she is on her way to a masked ball, tea at the Empress or a jaunt out to the country. I admire her panache and her

Author Cathy Converse interviewing Auntie Vie.
ROLF HICKER PHOTOGRAPHY

glitz—Auntie Vie loves glitz. She is the diva of fun and glitter.

As my kitchen window is angled toward hers, I am continually tormented by the magnificent aromas that pour forth from her stove. I am a writer and my hours don't fit into a normal day so I mostly snack; I rarely cook. If it weren't for my husband I would survive on tea and protein shakes. But when the scent of Auntie Vie's apple pie comes in through my window and the fragrance of cinnamon settles over me, I vow to do something about my cooking skills. I am not the only one affected. Auntie Vie's cooking revs up my dog's salivary glands. On warm days he sits outside on his small patch of grass staring intently at Auntie Vie's kitchen window as all two hundred million of his scent receptors twitch in anticipation. He casts a critical eye in my direction and heaves a sigh of displeasure at the lack of such deliciousness coming from our kitchen. He is ever hopeful.

Outside of her fashion and culinary skills, the thing that has impressed me the most is Auntie Vie's relationships with her family and friends. Being so close, I cannot help but hear the laughter that emanates from her direction. It is clear that she truly loves life, and obvious how much she loves people. There is always a car in her driveway belonging to a visiting family member or one of her friends; they are an important part of her life. No matter how busy members of her family are, they always take the time to stop in to see Auntie Vie. She is tremendously proud of them all and, at one time or another, many have lived with her. They drop in to share a day's event, their latest purchase or an award won. They come for a chat, to play cards or just to spend time. In return, they always get an emotional boost. Vie offers them a respite from their fast-paced lives. She listens, she does not advise, she does not scold; she brings them joy. She despairs that people no longer spend time with family or friends, that they have forgotten to stop for a moment, to breathe and to listen. Her heart extends to animals, too. She feeds strays and offers them shelter. She has housed rescued bunnies and nursed aging cats that came to her with barely enough skin to cover their bones—she loves them all.

In the course of working with Auntie Vie and chronicling her history, I came to understand her story as more than the study of one person. It is broader than that; it is a narrative of the Canadian experience. It is about the movement of people across the land, the settling of a new province and homesteading hardscrabble territory so future generations could prosper. It is also a story of the human condition: of coping and success, of fortitude and strength, and of sadness and great joy. Her history and that of others like her are the bedrock on which this nation was built.

This is not a book about aging, although Auntie Vie's age is obvious and she does offer up hints about growing older, generously sprinkled with humor. Auntie Vie would be awesome at any age. However, it is an inescapable fact that in another thirty years, the number of seniors in North America is expected to double and we will be in the midst of what some are calling a "longevity revolution." In our attempt to understand this new frontier, we have come to realize that aging is far more than the absence of illness; it is greatly affected by our lifestyle choices. Studies suggest that thirty per cent of aging is due to genetic factors, while a full seventy per cent is affected by our choices—how we age is within our control. While scientists edge closer to understanding the genetics of growing older, disease, disability, and other medical issues, it is on the area of lifestyle choices that we as individuals and communities need to focus. We all know that we must exercise, challenge our brains, eat right and maintain our social connections to live a healthy life. If we lose our sense of purpose, our wonderment, and our joy, it becomes all too easy to let those things go. Perhaps Auntie Vie's spunk and zest for life can serve as a lesson and inspire us all.

This is a book about one woman's joy and her passion for life. The format is like a scrapbook, with photos, illustrations of her clothing, and bits of advice scattered here and there rather than being presented in a highly organized linear fashion. Life does not always unfold in a neat and tidy manner, with our past behind us and our future yet to be; it flows around us, picking up various threads and dropping others as it narrates our story and weaves our perspective and our identity into the album that becomes our life.

Auntie Vie shares with us some of the threads that have shaped her life. She tells us of her history, which is at times both heartening and heartbreaking but always engaging. She models her fashion, talks about her love of shoes and jewelry, and shares some of her award-winning recipes. She offers us bits of wisdom and ideas on aging—often humorous—gleaned from living through eight decades. She asks that, in the process of your busy lives, you sometimes stop to enjoy it. "Remember, all life needs a little sparkle once in a while," she says.

Cathy Converse

Auntie Vie with a fresh batch of her pickles.
PHOTO COURTESY OF EILEEN ZAPSHALA

AUNTIE VIE'S
story

AUNTIE VIE'S
Childhood

November heralds the beginning of winter in Saskatchewan, when biting cold edges out the last vestiges of summer and hoarfrost quiets the busyness of the summer's activities. In the tiny village of Morse—five houses and one hospital—an infant lay crying in the arms of her mother. A big sister, who was miles away, was preparing for her wedding, but mother and babe would miss that celebration while they lay entwined in the newness of life.

This birth was the twelfth for Anna Friesen and her husband, Cornelius, and it was special. Vie was to be the youngest in their large family. A little boy with a big name like his father was born six years later, when Anna was forty-five, but he lived for only a month.

Vie did not start life with the name that was to become her signature identity. Anna could not decide what to name her new little daughter. She had already used Anna, Tina, Esther, Rose, Emily, and Luatta for her other daughters and she had simply run out of ideas. When it came time for Anna to sign the birth certificate, she asked the nurse what her name was.

"Eolia," the nurse said.

"Then I will give her the name of Eolia," but Anna added the biblical name of Sarah for the baby's middle name. Thus, her birth certificate states that Eolia Sarah Friesen was born on November 6, 1924.

Eolia was known by that name until she was fourteen and began working in a munitions plant in Ontario. Her co-workers and bosses found that Eolia was too difficult a name to shout out over the constant din of the factory's heavy machinery, so they called her Vie. Today, as matriarch of her family and to her many fans, she is known simply as Auntie Vie—a term of endearment and one of respect.

For the formative years of her life, Vie lived in Saskatchewan, a province noted for its big open skies and endless fields of golden wheat. "Our family was poor and for a while we lived like gypsies— we moved all over the place. Not all land was productive. Sometimes it was so dry and barren it was like the desert. You would pick a handful of soil up and it was just sand. You can't plant anything in that."

The remedy for baggy eyes **is either teabag poultices, Botox injections or sunglasses;** take your pick.

The late 1920s through to the end of the '30s were hard for farmers. The weather vacillated between extremes, from severe drought to crashing hailstorms, and crop failures became the norm. To add to the weather woes, the world was experiencing an unprecedented economic depression. Provincial income dropped by ninety per cent in Saskatchewan, families lost their farms, and there was little opportunity for work. Many walked away from their years of sweating over stubborn crops, but Vie's family stayed. They managed, but it was not easy.

"Dad was a thresher and had to go where the work was. We moved from Herbert and went east into

Manitoba to work in Gretna and Winkler, then back into Saskatchewan, traveling west to work in Swift Current, and later north into Biggar and Battleford. I was little so I don't remember much, but I can recall our moves. We traveled and lived on a hayrack; that's an open wagon that is used to load hay after it has been cut. Our lives revolved around that hayrack. Dad or my brothers hitched up the horses to the hayrack and we all piled in with all of our possessions and off we went. Mother had a big stove that seemed to dominant the hayrack, and that was where she cooked all of our meals and baked our bread. We killed the chickens for our suppers and milked the cow that walked along behind the hayrack. At nighttime we would snuggle down into our comforters and have a cozy sleep out under the stars, and when it rained we all huddled underneath the hayrack.

"On one of our moves, from Swift Current to Biggar, we met two men along the way who stayed with us for a while. I will never forget them. Captain Redcliff and Captain Leslie, from the Salvation Army, drove up in a big black Cadillac. They said they were hungry and wanted to know if they could share in our supper. We just stood there staring at the car. We had never seen anything like that car in our lives. We knew all about wagons, but not cars. It was like something from another world. Here we were—ten kids with our horses, a hayrack for a home and bare feet; we must have been quite a sight. We happily gave them dinner and afterwards sat around the campfire singing songs. Some of my brothers and sisters played instruments. I think we had an accordion, a mouth organ, and a banjo. They enjoyed themselves so much they stayed with us for a couple of days. That's how we were; we just had fun.

"We had a lot of music in our lives. My sister Rosie played the xylophone, the saxophone, the accordion and an old French horn, Esther played the trumpet, my brother played the mouth organ and the banjo, and we all sang. I couldn't play any instruments but I loved to sing—I sang in the church choir. We never had lessons, there was not any money for that kind of thing; we made our own music. People were always coming over to our house and they would bring their banjos and guitars and we would have such fun."

After living the life of an itinerant farm family, Vie's parents finally settled in Battleford near the site that had been the center of the 1885 Northwest Rebellion. Battleford is in west-central Saskatchewan on the North Saskatchewan River, seventy-five miles farther north than the family had ever been and more than two hundred miles from the place of Vie's birth in Morse.

"We eventually settled in North Battleford. We sort of stumbled into home ownership. There was a five-room log cabin owned by some man, I don't know who he was. Anyway, he really wanted my brother's gun, so they cut a deal. Pete traded the gun for the house. I don't know what guns cost today but I do know what log houses cost—I still can't believe we got a house for a gun. I guess my parents thought it was a good deal but we kids were so embarrassed by that house. When we had our friends over we never took them into the house; we would go to the barn instead. We had the only log house around. Our dream was to have a clapboard house like everybody else.

"It was a big house, though. The inside walls were covered with beaverboard and the floors were laid with wide-planked wood. I remember scrubbing those floors with lye soap until they were spotless. That lye soap sure took the skin off my hands. It had a very pungent, sharp odor, but it was the smell of clean for us. We used three of the rooms for our bedrooms. Mother made us lovely warm blankets to sleep under. She used the wool from our sheep, carded and somehow compacted into large squares, which she then stitched together into a quilt. Our furniture was pretty basic. The only nice piece of furniture we had was a radio; it was battery operated. My brother Pete bought it. It was in a big beautiful case. I used to love listening to the programs. *Amos 'n' Andy*, a comedy show, was one of the most popular.

"Our bathroom was an outhouse. When it snowed, my brothers had to keep the path to the outhouse cleared. Can you imagine one bathroom for all those people? There was never a line-up, though, because you didn't want to be hopping up and down in freezing cold winter temperatures for long. When you see

Dad always said, **"Be kind to old people,"** because we will all get old one day.

snow devils whipping around and snow nearly covering the barn, how long are you going to take? For our baths, Mother would get a big bucket of snow and then melt it on the stove. Then she would fill up a large tub that she put in the kitchen, which was the warmest part of the house. We would scrub ourselves until we were pink. Mother made all of our soap. I don't know the exact recipe, but she used water, lye, and lard. We may have been the poorest kids at school but we were told we were the cleanest. Mother washed all our clothes and linens by hand. She had a bucket and a washboard that she scrubbed the clothes on. I really don't know how she did it, with all of cooking, cleaning, knitting, and taking care of all of us kids—she never complained.

"As time went on, Dad bought up more land until we had a small ranch. We grew all of our vegetables. We

stored our root vegetables in the root cellar and we canned and pickled a lot of our vegetables and fruits for the winter. We had thirty acres of garden that we all tended. In the summers, Dad would sit out on the porch as we girls weeded the garden, and if we missed one weed he was sure to tell us about it. Our garden was beautiful. We grew great big watermelons that were deliciously succulent. As soon as the first one appeared we would pick it and immediately slice into it. In no time at all, we had pink juice running down our arms and bits of watermelon and black seeds stuck to our faces. There was nothing better.

"We had pumpkins, peppers, celery, cabbage, cauliflower, broccoli, carrots, turnips, lettuce, tomatoes—everything that would grow in our climate was in our garden. The rows of vegetables were so straight that people used to come from miles around to take pictures. We had cows, chickens, fifty turkeys, horses, sheep, and a few goats. The goats were pets for us to play with. We all worked. My brother Pete taught me how to drive the John Deere tractor when I was just ten. I don't think my mother approved, but I loved it. I didn't always tell her when I was driving the tractor but I would come back into the house looking like I had been in a dust storm and she would get after my brothers for letting me drive it.

"I used to walk to school but I was not very big and it was hard sometimes, walking in the snow. I never complained but the teacher would see how cold I was and she would put me on her lap and hold me to warm me up. She said to Dad one time that I was too little to be walking that distance in the snow and that he needed to think of another way for me to get there. He carried me to school for a while and then he got me a little black-and-white Shetland pony to ride. His name was Billy. Our big horse was named Billy, too. Anyway, I rode little Billy every day to my school; it was about two miles from home. Every morning before I left I would put a bale of hay on Billy's back to take to school for him. The school had a caretaker that fed our horses the hay we brought and made sure they were well watered.

"Dad spoiled my little pony. When we came home from school he always had a sugar cube ready for Billy. Billy looked forward to his afternoon treat and as soon as we were close to home he would break out into a trot. I kept telling Dad not to feed him because it wasn't good for him. Billy got so fat from those sugar cubes that I had trouble staying on him.

"Our school was a huge, red-brick building—Kings Street School it was called. All the kids from around North Battleford went there. It covered all of the grades from one to twelve. Our teachers were really strict and if you misbehaved you got the strap. I think it was 'Rule kids by fear.' It was very effective but sometimes, even despite the threat of punishment, we just couldn't help ourselves. I was pretty good and didn't get into much trouble but I remember one incident when the teacher sent me outside to ring the cowbell to bring everyone in from recess—we didn't have a buzzer so we used a cowbell and I was the cowbell ringer.

"I went out and rang the bell and a bunch of the kids, including my brother Jake, defied the rules and jumped on a toboggan and took one more ride down the hill. They knew they were going to get heck, but sometimes you just have to do something like that. It took them half an hour to walk back up the hill. The teacher was waiting for them when they got back and was she mad! She lined them all up and told them to hold out their hands, palms facing down, and she strapped each one of them. It was a menacing, big rubber strap made out of an old tire. Everyone winced when she brought that strap down. You could hear it bite into their frozen hands. It sure tore their skin up. Jake had to hide his hands when we got home that afternoon or Dad would have strapped him again. There was no sympathy.

"Winters in North Battleford were long and cold. The temperature would get down to minus twenty degrees Fahrenheit or colder—sometimes it would reach minus sixty degrees. The prairie wind would sweep over the land freezing everything in its path, especially any skin we had exposed, like our ears, noses, and fingers. We always had to be careful of frostbite. We wore hats and mittens that Mother knitted for us, and wool scarves that we wrapped around our faces to protect our lungs. Walking two miles in snow takes some effort so we would huff and pant and by the time we got to school we would be covered in white frost from the heat escaping from our bodies. We looked like snowmen. The one thing that you did not want to do was to get sick in the winter. The nearest doctor was fifteen miles away. One winter I got really sick. I don't remember what was wrong but I had foam coming out of my mouth.

Socialize with young people.
They are full of life and energy.
Old people can be depressing.

Everyone thought I was going to die so my dad got the horses hooked up to the cutter and took me to the doctor.

"Winter would start in November, although it was cold and frosty in September. We didn't have electricity that you could switch on or heaters that could be turned up with the twist of a dial. We used coal-oil lamps for our light. The light was not the brightest light—it glowed a dull, orangey-yellow color—but it made you feel snug and cozy. Mother would sit in her chair by the light and mend or knit under the flickering flame. Much later, we got a mantle lamp, which gave a much brighter light. We had to be very careful around it because the gas that it used was combustible and it released carbon monoxide into the air, so you never left it unattended.

"Our main source of heat came from our potbelly stove. You never wanted to let the fire burn out in that stove or you would freeze. The stove had to be stoked all day and all night. Mother and Dad would take shifts; Mother took the day shift and Dad took the night shift. He stayed up all night putting logs on the fire to keep us warm. He would sleep during the day. We always had a great big pile of wood that we kids had chopped. That potbelly stove warmed the whole cabin."

AUNTIE VIE'S
Family

Vie's parents and grandparents were pioneers, farmers who chiseled away at the bald prairie land to bring shape and prosperity to a newly minted province. On September 1, 1905, Saskatchewan officially became a province of the Dominion of Canada. The young province needed people who were willing to work hard and had generations of farming experience behind them, proven farmers from another country, perhaps. Canada developed one of the most successful advertising campaigns in its history, touting the natural beauty and vastness of the land, and the opportunities available to those who would settle the West. As an extra incentive, the government promised a quarter section of land—one hundred and sixty acres—for the small administrative fee of ten dollars. The Dominion Lands Act stipulated that in order to keep the land, a permanent building needed to be constructed and at least forty acres had to be cultivated within three years.

Mennonites were high on the list of prospective home-steaders; they had first settled in Upper Canada in 1776 and were known to be excellent farmers. The problem was that they lived in established communities in Russia and were not likely to immigrate as individual families. Clifford Sifton, the federal Minister of the Interior under

Canadian Prime Minister Sir Wilfrid Laurier, appealed to them by granting sections of land to which they could move their entire communities. Mennonites had been this route before and wanted certain guarantees, such as freedom from military service, freedom of worship, and independence from the government. Federal government officials agreed and, to make the move easier, they subsidized the ocean passage from Europe and provided help with transportation in Canada.

It was a successful campaign; between 1896 and 1905, hundreds of thousands of Eastern European immigrants came to the West. In his later years, describing the quality of immigrant he was looking for, Sifton said, "I think that a stalwart peasant in a sheepskin coat, born on the soil, whose forefathers have been farmers for ten generations, with a stout wife and a half-dozen children, is good quality."

Vie's family was exactly the type of people that Sifton had in mind; they believed in self-reliance, had a strong community identity, were peaceable, had an established reputation of good works, and were proven farmers. They were not, however, peasants; they did not wear sheepskin coats, nor were they stout. Jacob and Katarina Schultz, Vie's maternal grandparents, had been prosperous farmers in Russia and were able to buy their children luxuries. Although certainly stalwart in energy and heart, Katarina was a tiny woman.

Vie's mother and grandmother were both Mennonites and Vie herself was baptized in the glacier-fed waters of the South Battleford River. She remembers her initiation clearly. "I'll never forget my baptism. We stood on the banks of the South Battleford and looked out over this long flowing river, the very same river that freezes in the winter. It might be nice for the geese and ducks,

I thought, but it didn't look very inviting for me. I just closed my eyes and walked in. I know we were expected to be focusing on the more spiritual side of life. This was supposed to be an intensely emotional experience. It was an important rite of passage in which we were to be reborn into a new spiritual life. But let me tell you, that water was so cold all I could think about was if I don't get out of here I am going to turn into an ice block—dunk and run was all that was on my mind."

Some Mennonite groups live in closed communities, apart from the world, others in more open communities and a few, like Vie's family, are scattered throughout the general population. For Vie, circumstances created a drift away from her earlier roots and, as an adult, she had little opportunity to maintain her Mennonite way of life, although her faith is intact and she took her daughter to church and Sunday school regularly.

Anna, Vie's mother, was born in Russia and immigrated to Canada with her parents in 1901, when she was sixteen. Slavic resentment toward the Mennonites was becoming more virulent and threatening, and Anna's parents felt they had no choice but to leave the comfortable life they had in Russia. Deep within the vault of the family's memory is that something had happened in Russia that caused Jacob and Katarina Schultz to gather their children and leave their house and all of their possessions under cover of darkness. Perhaps they foresaw what was to come. During the lead-up to the First World War, the abdication of Tsar Nicholas II in 1917, and the establishment of the Russian Republic, chaos reigned throughout Russia, and Mennonites, who were perceived to be more prosperous than the average peasant, were targeted with

Love people and help people; be kind and loving.

hostilities. They were murdered, their women and young girls were raped, and entire villages were destroyed. By that time, Anna and her family were safe in their new country.

> It's not about money—it's so cold.
> **You can't cuddle up to money**
> but you can cuddle up to people.

The family's trip from Russia to England took about eighteen days, during which time Anna became quite ill. When they arrived in Liverpool, she was immediately taken to the hospital and the doctors said she was too ill to travel on to Québec. The family had to leave her at the hospital. When she was better, they told her, she should book passage on another ship and they would meet her in Canada. It was a long six weeks before Anna saw her family again.

After they arrived in Québec, the family boarded one of the old, wooden "Colonist Cars," which were former first-class railcars rebuilt by the Canadian Pacific Railway to carry the many immigrants who were going to the prairies. The cars were crowded, uncomfortable, and lacked privacy, and Anna's family must have wondered if they had made the right decision in coming to this strange, faraway country. The trip to the western edge of the Red River valley took them seven days.

Their destination was Winkler, Manitoba, a small village peopled mostly by Germans, Russian Mennonites, and Central Europeans. Anna's family took some comfort in the knowledge that there had been Mennonite settlements in Winkler as early as 1874; they would not be alone. However, things don't always work out as anticipated and they found that most of the prime farmland had already been claimed. Securing a homestead was not as easy as they had been led to believe.

By the summer of 1903, land was available around

Herbert, in a vast territory of wild prairie land in the southwest part of Saskatchewan. Mennonites from Winkler were offered round-trip transportation, food, and lodging for an exploratory excursion to Herbert—all for the price of ten dollars—and more than a hundred men accepted the offer. The area was shocking in its starkness. There was not a house to be found nor a person to be seen; they had only the wildlife and the pesky prairie mosquito to keep them company. Herbert was very different from their settled communities in Russia, with its gardens, schools, factories, and established homes, but the land offered limitless potential to those with knowledge of farming and willingness to work hard.

Up to this point, Vie's grandparents had spent three years on the move and they were anxious to put down roots; they were among the first pioneers to settle in Herbert. When they got there, they immediately set out across the land, traveling north and east, looking for suitable acreage that would support them. Eventually, they filed papers for a quarter section of land north of the town.

The "town" had only a boxcar that served as the rail station, but within a year there was a small store, a real estate office, an accountant, and a café. By 1906, there were fifty farms in the area and by 1911 they had a newspaper, two lumber yards, an airfield, two doctors, three hotels, a racetrack, and a popcorn stand. In time, Herbert developed a robust Mennonite presence.

The Schultzes were experienced in farming, and breaking virgin ground was not new to them; still, it was a daunting task that lay before them. They had no wells on their land so they had to haul water in buckets and on carts from a slough nearby. They were too poor to buy machinery so they worked their land by hand, harvesting their crops with a scythe and threshing the grain on a rock. They were racing against time for they had to have forty acres under plough within three years. Working hard, they were able to break about ten to twenty acres a year. They sowed crops of oats, flax and wheat.

Two years after settling onto their new land, Anna's family had built a sturdy, two-storey, wood-frame, clapboard house. Despite their difficulties, by all accounts their home was a happy one, where people came to gather, to laugh, and to support each other. It was in this house that Anna and Vie's father, Cornelius Friesen, were married in 1906. Anna's wedding was the first for the small settlement of Mennonites; she was twenty-one and her husband was twenty-two.

Vie, on the right, and her sister-in-law Leaha were bored picking apples for the Okanagan Packing Plant, so they made themselves Hawaiian grass skirts and danced.

AUNTIE VIE'S
Early Life

Vie's early life was not much different from her mother's. In Russia, Anna's family had looked down on the peasants who were seen as vulgar and uneducated, and whose morals seemed depraved. While her family's financial fortunes were not what they once were, Anna took her responsibilities very seriously. She raised her children with pride and taught them to be ethical and virtuous. She spoke her ancestral languages, German and Dutch, to her children, and she was deeply conscientious about imparting her family's theology to them.

"Mother was very religious," Vie explains, "and, like her, I was raised as a Mennonite. We went to church, every Sunday but because we often lived in places where there were no Mennonite services, we went to whatever church was nearby. When we did go to a Mennonite church, the thing I remember most was the singing. The women had this melancholic sound but sang as if they were one voice. It was pure bliss—the music would just float out of the church. They sang a cappella, without instruments. The hymns were very historical and they sang them the way they had always been sung throughout time.

"Religious instruction was very important to Mother and every morning before we went to school and every evening before supper, all of my brothers and sisters would gather together and Mother would read a chapter of the Bible. For her, the Scriptures were the ultimate guides on how life should be lived. The evening Bible reading was hard for us because we would come home from school so hungry, and the smell of roast chicken and the yeasty scent of hot fresh buns made it impossible for us to focus on anything but our stomachs. I don't think I ever heard a word of what she read; all I could think about was that delicious food cooking in the oven. Honest to goodness, it was enough to turn you off religion."

Mennonite child rearing was very strict and focused on unquestioned obedience that was backed up by a firm hand for misbehavior. "Both my mother and father were very strict. If we didn't behave, we would get the strap. I didn't get many lickings—I was the youngest and Dad was more lenient with me. If any of us got in trouble at school, no one would say anything to Dad because he would get out his strap and we would get it again. We cut a big path around our dad. I was kind of afraid of him. We girls couldn't wear make-up or curl our hair and when Dad said to be in at seven o'clock he meant 'seven o'clock,' not one minute after. He had seven girls and he said, 'if any of you girls go and get pregnant, that will be the end of you.' That was the best birth control pill there was, not that we really knew what that was all about. Parents didn't talk openly to their kids about such serious matters. I was married two years before I understood what it was all about. I thought, hell, this is no damn good. I'm surprised that my husband stayed with me.

"Even though my parents were strict and times were hard, we had a lot of fun. I think we had more fun than kids today. In the winter, we would hitch up our horses, Billy and Patty, to the cutter—it's like a sleigh—and we would put heated rocks under our blankets to keep us warm. We rode through the fields, bells jingling and the cold air stinging our faces. Sometimes we were accompanied by the Northern Lights, shimmering green, indigo, or blood red; it was magical.

"Several times a year, we would get about thirty or forty people together and have a barn dance. They were so much fun. We had music, singing, and dancing—I lived for dancing. We had a large, red barn and we would hold the dance on the top floor. All of the cows and horses were below us, tucked safely in their stalls. People came prepared to spend the night because it was too far for anyone to get home in the dark, and it was too cold for the horses. As people came, they unhitched their horses and brought them into the barn to keep them warm. All of the sleighs would be lined up outside and Dad would make sure they were covered with blankets to keep the snow out. Standing outside looking into the barn, you could see the golden glow of light through the cracks and hear the music and the dancing echoing out from the top floor. It all made your heart pump a little bit faster.

"I don't think there is anything better than a good, old-fashioned barn dance. We never had to worry about how loud our music was because there was no one around to be bothered by it. We made our own music, mostly country and western. Some of my brothers and sisters would play, as well as some of the guests, who brought their own instruments. We generally had a mouth organ, a banjo, an accordion, a guitar, and a piano. You could really get a beat going with all of those instruments. Mother wouldn't come because she didn't believe in dancing

Sing, dance, laugh, **be joyful, bring joy, love—** it's a great adventure.

herself, but she would make us homemade bread and delicious cinnamon buns that smelled so good. We had plates of our homemade smoked sausages and coffee that was kept warm on the potbelly stove. Outside it may have been cold and snowing but inside we danced up a storm. Maybe we didn't have the best of clothes and shoes but we forgot about that when we danced.

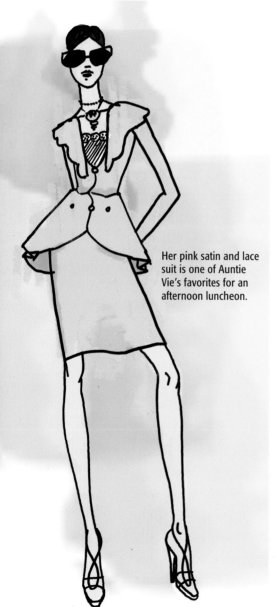

Her pink satin and lace suit is one of Auntie Vie's favorites for an afternoon luncheon.

"After a long, hard winter we looked forward to spring. In Saskatchewan, winter ends one day and spring starts the next. When the ice began to break up on the river, we knew it was spring, which meant that it was time for our annual spring rite of riding the ice floes downstream. As soon as we heard that first crack we would run up the river, choose an ice floe and take one almighty leap, hoping the ice wouldn't flip over on us. We never told our mother. There are just some things you don't tell your parents.

"From the beginning of spring to about September we would get these terrible, loud, crashing, ear-shattering thunderstorms, and with thunderstorms you always get lightning. During one particularly bad storm, Mother came upstairs to gather us together and bring us down to the main floor because, she said, if lightning struck the house we would be trapped. We were all huddled up downstairs counting the seconds before each boom—*one* one-thousand, *two* one-thousand—when all of a sudden I saw a flash hit the window and then there was a loud crash. Lightning struck our bay window, shattering the glass all over. It streaked across the floor faster than you could blink and disappeared out the other side of the house. I was standing up on a chair as it sped right past me. It was a good thing, otherwise I would have been directly in its path. We were lucky no one was hurt.

"There was another time when my sister and I had gone to bring the cows and horses in from the paddock. As we were walking toward the field, the sky was darkening and the clouds were piling up higher and higher. We were in for a thunderstorm. We figured we didn't have time to walk the long way around to the gate, so we took a shortcut. We dropped down onto our stomachs and slipped under the barbed-wire fence, not exactly the place you want to be when lightning strikes. Just as we were crawling under the fence, we heard a big boom and a streak of lightning grazed right over our backs. We were lucky that time, too. You know the old saying, 'It's about as likely to happen as being stuck by lightning'? I am terrified of lightning.

"The summers were a busy time for us. We had to plant our crops as well as our garden and we had to keep the garden free of weeds; we fed the animals and milked the cows—all the things you need to do to keep a farm going. We also had our household chores to attend to— washing, cleaning, sewing, baking, canning, pickling. Mother canned all of our meats. We had chicken, beef, turkey, and duck. She would boil the meat for five or six hours in a big double boiler. I can still taste it. The meat was very tender and it melted in your mouth. For our suppers she would make gravy to go over the meat and boil up some of our garden potatoes. The potatoes we had on the prairies were exceptionally sweet, not like the watery ones we have here. We made our own jellies and jams. We didn't grow much fruit but we would pick wild blueberries and chokecherries. You had to take the seeds out of the chokecherries because they were poisonous. We would go on wild strawberry hunts and collect as many berries as we could find and bring them home to our mother. She would make us strawberry shortcake and we would cover it with our own thick cream.

"During harvest time, my sisters and I would help stook the sheaves of hay and wheat. We would run along behind the binder, which bundled and tied the hay into sheaves, and we would pick up the sheaves and lean them upright against each other until they resembled a pyramid. The stooks were taller than we were. It was hard work because we had to get the stooks just right so enough air would flow through the sheaves to dry them properly. If we did our job right, the outside of the stooks might weather but the insides would be waterproof. If hay is too moist it will get musty and moldy and won't be any good and will make the animals sick. When we were finished, I don't think you could tell the difference between a stook and us, because we probably had as much wheat on us as in those piles of sheaves. Every once in a while, I get a whiff of something that reminds me of those days. I will never forget the scent of freshly cut hay; it has a special perfume all its own. It smells like sheets that have been drying out on the clothesline; crisp, clean—it's the smell of summer. Sometimes in the evenings there would be a pink glow on the horizon that made everything look soft and delicate; it was a beautiful sight to look out over the fields and see long rows of triangular-shaped stooks of hay dotting the pasture.

"When our chores were done for the day, we would all get together—Dad, too—and play baseball; there were certainly enough of us. We sang, we danced, and sometimes we played whist in the evening. Those were great moments. You take a lot of those little moments and you put them together and suddenly you have a whole lot of great things that you can wrap up in your memories. Life is not about material things, it never has been; it's about all of those special moments."

Don't judge people. You don't know what they have been through.

When the Second World War broke out, over one million women worked in the Canadian war production industry, seventy-five thousand of them in munitions factories. The United States had "Rosie the Riveter" but Canada had "Ronnie the Bren Gun Girl," the poster girl representing women's work for the war effort. Vie was one of the young women who answered the call to work.

"I didn't want to be a burden on my parents and the war plants were gearing up. I knew it was time I earned my own way in the world. I was hired to work at a munitions plant in Woodstock, Ontario. The government paid for my train fare and meals, and I had saved up my money and had fifteen dollars in my pocket. I thought I was rich. I got on the train bound for Toronto. It was exciting because this was the first time I had ever been away from home. I was dressed in a nice pair of slacks and a new shirt. We were given meal tickets to use on the train. There were two classes of dining cars, one for us and one for the soldiers. Our tickets were worth five dollars and with that we would get pancakes, bacon and eggs, and coffee. The soldiers who were going to fight in the war for us were treated shabbily as far as food went. Their meal tickets were for a dollar only. I was homesick already and couldn't eat so I gave my meal tickets to them. We were also given vouchers for liquor and I didn't drink, of course, so I gave those to the soldiers, too. They were so happy and it made me feel good that I could do something for them.

"The reality of leaving home set in when I arrived in Toronto. I had to find my way to Woodstock. There were eleven trains going every which way and I had to figure out which trains were going where and then get to the one I was supposed to be on. There were no information booths anywhere to guide me. I'm telling you, that was something else. I felt like a little waif. I was only fourteen years old, a rural farm girl, and I was suddenly thrust into an adult, urban world. When I got to Woodstock, it was five o'clock in the afternoon. I had no place to go so I bought a newspaper and looked for a boarding house. There was a room advertised for thirty-five dollars a month. I picked up my suitcase and found my way to the address that was listed in the paper. As luck would have it, the owner said I could move in right away. I think my confidence started growing right then. I had done something that was way beyond any of my experiences and I had succeeded.

"My job with the war works started the very next day. When I put on my new work uniform, I felt very proud. The coveralls that we wore were actually quite smart looking. There were five hundred young women working at the war plant. There were very few men except for our bosses; most of the men were away fighting in the war. Apparently, the wages paid to the men were higher than ours. It was said they had to take care of their families. I think some women were angry but I never really gave

Her black silk dress with gold lamé trim and gold shoes is one of Auntie Vie's favorite outfits for an evening of cocktails.

it much thought. I had never had a paycheck before so I had nothing to compare it with. My job was to run the base recess machines. We were making shells for bombs and the part I worked with was the base, or the bottom, of the shell. When the shells came to me, they weighed seventy-five pounds. I only weighed ninety-five pounds myself, not a particularly good ratio, I guess, but that was the job. The part of the shell that I dealt with was the inch-diameter base that was recessed into the bottom. It was the bit that was filled with gunpowder.

"The second day into my job, a guy dropped one of the five-hundred-pound shells on my foot. I was wearing steel-capped boots but the bomb crushed my shoe and the steel from the reinforced toecap dug right into my foot. I was laid up for six weeks. My boss asked me to come into work anyway, although he said I didn't have to work. I was told that the company would continue to pay my full wages. That sounded pretty good to me, even though I have never been one to sit around. Apparently he didn't want me to go onto Workmen's Compensation. I was young and really didn't understand how all of the bureaucracy worked or what my entitlements were, so I hobbled into work every day with my crutches.

"I was still homesick and pretty lonely so my sisters Rosie and Larry, who were working in Toronto at the time, came to get me to take me back to live with them, but the munitions plant wouldn't let me go. They said I was a good worker and they didn't want to lose me. They also reminded me that I had signed a contract and couldn't leave in any case. I had no option but to stay. I think one of my sisters said to my boss that he was running the place like a prison. I would have loved to go with them but I did like my job. I ended up working at the war plant for six years.

"The work we were doing was dangerous and we always had to be careful. We were working with a lot of big machinery and with explosives. One of the things we had to do was wear caps to cover our hair. They weren't unattractive; in fact they were surprisingly appealing. One day, one of the girls came to work and had not tucked her bangs under her hat. She was very pretty and said she was tired of always sticking all of her hair under the cap and she thought it would be okay to have a bit of hair showing. We were busy working and all of a sudden we heard this awful scream. I had never heard anything like that before. Her bangs had somehow become entangled in the machine and ripped her scalp right off. She passed out and died right there. We were stunned. A hush went out over the whole factory floor. Most of us had never seen an accident like that before; it made me sick to my stomach.

Accessorize your outfits.
Pearls are classy.

"It was hard to pick up and work after that but the soldiers needed our products and the war wasn't going to stop because we had had a tragic accident. We were all aware of the dangers of the job, but you never think anything like that will ever happen. After they removed her body, the boss came to me and asked if I would clean the machine where she had been working because he needed it up and running right away. There was blood and hair everywhere. I dug in my heels and said, 'I am not doing that. You can fire me if you want, but I am not cleaning that machine.' That was not the only serious accident.

"There was another time when fifteen girls were killed when the part of the plant they were working in exploded. I was working in the building next door. We all heard the explosion. The blast shook everything. We dropped what we were doing and ran out and then saw the building on fire. That was a terrible accident; it shook me to the core. Accidents like that didn't happen very often but when they did, it was devastating. We knew those women; they were young and full of life and had ambitions just like the rest of us. It could have been any one of us. It changes your perspective pretty fast on what is important. I think that is in part what motivates me to live life to the fullest. Life is so precious, you don't want to waste a minute of it.

"One of the other jobs I did while working at the munitions plant was to fold parachutes. We had to really concentrate on what we were doing because if we didn't fold them just right, we knew that a soldier could die. Their lives were in our hands. It was a big responsibility and pretty intense work. Sometimes we would get parachutes that were ripped or had holes in them, and we were allowed to take them home and sew dresses out of the silk. We made some lovely clothes out of that material.

"When I went to work in Woodstock, I had not yet finished high school so I took night school until I had my Grade 13. I would work from noon to eight in the evening and then I would go back to my room and sleep for a few hours and then get up and go to school. Looking back, I don't know how I did it, but when you're young you have energy to burn.

"After I finished my contract with the munitions plant, I went to Toronto and worked for General Electric. I made coils for neon signs. My sisters were still in Toronto so I was not as lonely anymore. I was working at GE when the war ended. I remember when we heard about the end of the war in Europe. It was May 7, 1945, and V-E Day was to be declared the next day. The city went wild. People held up newspapers with headlines that read 'Hitler Gives Up.' Allied flags snapped in the breeze, church bells rang out, car horns were honking, thousands of people poured out into the streets from their factories and offices, and the sky rained confetti. Years of tension were released by dancing and singing on the streets. You could hear 'O Canada' being sung above the noise. It was a spontaneous, jubilant celebration. We all knew that the war in the Pacific was ongoing (it would not be over for another four months), but for right now, V-E Day was victory enough for us."

AUNTIE VIE
Moves West

"I had been working at General Electric for a year, but when the war ended I wanted to go home. I just had a sense that something was going to happen to my dad or my mother. My sister tried to persuade me to stay, because I was making good money and I wasn't going to be laid off. With the soldiers returning home and needing jobs, many women were laid off work, and my sister was afraid that if I gave up my job, I wouldn't be able to find another one. But I just couldn't get rid of that impending sense of doom I had. Maybe it was a premonition, because I was home for only two months when my dad passed away. He died of a heart attack quite unexpectedly.

"I don't know what my mother would have done if I hadn't been there. She had no way to contact anybody, because there was no telephone and we didn't have a car. I went to get the preacher to come and help me with my dad. We hitched up the horses and got Dad's body onto the hayrack and took him to the funeral parlor in North Battleford. He was quite young, only sixty-two. I suspect that Dad might have had heart problems because he was always so pale. I don't think he had been to the doctor, not that it would have mattered much. In those days the doctors didn't tell you what was wrong

Vie and her mother around 1946, shortly after Vie's father died.
FAMILY PHOTO

or what changes you were supposed to make in your life if something was wrong. Dad had slowed down before his heart attack. He had given up farming and was working at the Weyburn Mental Hospital in Battleford. I know many of the mental hospitals at the time were pretty bleak places but Weyburn wasn't like that; it was one of the most progressive mental hospitals in the country. They had cutting-edge treatments and were known for their psychiatric drug research. It was a good place to work and I think Dad enjoyed it. My dad worked so darn hard all of his life—I suspect that was what probably killed him.

"When Dad died, I had been working as a government inspector, grading eggs—that was an interesting job. I had to make sure all proper sanitation and operating requirements were met and check that the eggs were accurately weighed and graded. I also worked as a government safety inspector for poultry. I had saved a fair amount of money from my previous jobs and I had a big paycheck coming. I also had a number of fifty-dollar Victory bonds that I had won in the work pools we had going at the munitions plant. Actually, I won the pool five times in a row until they said I couldn't enter anymore. The bonds paid a small rate of interest, something like one or one-and-a-half per cent, I can't remember exactly. Anyway, I gave my mother all of my money and asked her what she wanted to do. She said that she wanted to get as far away from North Battleford as she could. So I gave notice to my employers and Mother and I boarded a train and took off to British Columbia.

"We didn't really know anyone in British Columbia. There was a large Mennonite community in Abbotsford, which would be a comfort to Mother. We lived by ourselves for a while and later quite a number of our relatives followed. I was working to support us. Fortunately, I never had trouble finding a job. In fact, about two days after we arrived in Abbotsford I had a job as a government food inspector. I worked long hours. My usual working days were sixteen hours, sometimes longer. I worked at night as a government inspector and during the day I picked strawberries, apples, raspberries, and peaches. Many times I worked straight through the night with one job and then all day with the other job. I needed to earn enough money to build us a small house.

> Don't brood.
> **The next best thing may be** just around the corner.

"When that day finally came, I went out and bought all of the building materials for our house. It was very exciting to think that we were finally going to get our own place. Mother was connected to the church and in the best of community spirit, the preacher gathered together a number of the men and they built our little house. It was a wonderful house. Mother had a beautiful garden and people were always stopping by to admire her roses and her poppies. Life went on quite nicely. I worked and Mother tended her garden. Then, some years after my father died, my mother married his brother."

It was not uncommon among immigrant communities for families to take care of each other when a spouse died, so it would have been quite natural for Anna to marry her brother-in-law. Vie's uncle had an interesting history himself. Peter Friesen, like his brother, had been born in Manitoba; their parents had emigrated from Russia in 1874. They were raised in Mennonite communities, although Vie's father was not particularly religious. Peter, however, was very active in his church. At one point he left Canada and took a trainload of

Mennonites to Mexico to help establish a colony there. Around 1922, twenty thousand Canadian Mennonites left their farms and their home country and immigrated to Mexico, because they felt that their way of life in Canada was under attack.

In the early 1920s, the Mexican government wanted to settle the northern part of Mexico, around Chihuahua, and they looked to the Mennonites as good farmers who would work the land and make it blossom. Mexican president Álvaro Obergón promised the Mennonites they could maintain their way of life as they had done for centuries, provided inexpensive land for them, and granted them a one-hundred-year exemption from taxation. All the Mennonites had to do was farm the land and provide northern Mexico with their famous cheese, Queso Menonita.

Peter eventually returned to Canada to help his deceased brother's wife, and he and Anna were married in the Mennonite Brethren Church in Clearbrook in 1952. Unfortunately for Anna, he died five years later of a heart attack, the same condition that had taken his brother. He died during the month of June in 1957. Before Peter died, Anna wrote in her diary:

April 17, 1957
It is a nice day and again we are one day nearer to eternity. Oh be wise, only once do you make this journey, leave a good testimony behind. Let us live each day as if the day is the last day . . . time is so short and then is the long eternity.

May 14, 1957
Today is May 14, yesterday the 13th of May we received the message that my brother died. Therefore

we are now a brother and three sisters. How long we live we don't know but one thing we know that we have a home in heaven where there will be not parting and no more suffering. That will be glorious and wonderful. But as long as we live on earth we are to work, be ambitious and busy so we can help the poor. That is what the dear Lord wants of us although I have failed in this also.

Vie's mother lived another twenty-four years. She was ninety-six when she passed away, leaving a rich legacy tied to the history of a developing nation. It was people like Anna who played an important part in helping a new province and a young country reach their potential. As she nourished the land through her hard work, so too did she nourish a country's dreams.

"Mother had a clear mind right until the very end. I don't know how my mother and father did what they did. They both worked really hard. My mother was a loveable little person; even after having all of those children, she smiled and laughed a lot and missed all of her kids. I couldn't imagine having as many children as she did. In fact, after just one child, I told my husband to get the heck out of the nursery, I didn't want to see him. I was teasing, of course, but thirteen children—how did she do that? She was only four feet nine inches and weighed one hundred and ten pounds. I don't know where her physical strength came from."

When Vie felt that her mother was suitably looked after, she finally agreed to marry her long-time suitor.

"Len Zapshala and I had known each other for a number of years—we had quite a prolonged courtship. Len was very persistent. He kept proposing to me but my response was always the same: I had to take care of my

Vie and Len on their wedding day.
FAMILY PHOTO

mother. He waited four years for me. We were married
at the end of March in 1950. I had a lovely wedding.
I guess even then weddings were all about the brides and
their gowns."

Wedding dresses in the 1950s were very elegant and
ultra feminine. It was the first time since the Second
World War that designers and dressmakers could break
out of the fabric restrictions imposed on them by ration-
ing—and they did. Bridal gowns were often twenty-five
yards of pure scrumptiousness.

"I remember my wedding dress. I felt like a princess that day. My gown was so feminine. It was a Hollywood creation and the material was slipper satin and lace; it was a long gown that draped over a hoop skirt. The bodice was fitted and had dainty, lily point sleeves. The skirt portion of my dress was layered with tiers and tiers of imported lace that had pearls and rosettes appliquéd onto it. My headpiece was a tiara that was studded with rhinestones, and attached to that was a cathedral-length tulle veil that draped around me. The edges at the bottom of the veil were scalloped and had satin leaves appliquéd on them. I carried a large bouquet of deep pink roses that were seated in a bed of lush ferns that cascaded down dainty ribbons. Len was so handsome and looked sophisticated and elegant in his suit. He had beautiful curly blond hair—how could I resist him?"

Before Vie and Len, met he had been a Chief Petty Officer serving aboard the HMCS *Athabaskan*, one of the Tribal-class destroyers of the Royal Canadian Navy. The ship and Len had quite an extraordinary history together. The *Athabaskan* seemed to be a doomed ship even before it began its service: it had sustained bomb damage while it was under construction in the United Kingdom and was in two minor collisions. During Len's service aboard, the ship was the target of two different torpedo incidents, the first in the Bay of Biscay in the summer of 1943.

Always give a thought **to putting some sparkle** in your life.

Twenty German aircraft suddenly swooped down from the sky and pandemonium reigned as bombs dropped all over. The *Athabaskan* received a direct hit by one of the new German Henschel glider bombs. The bomb penetrated the hull, passing through the chart house and the Petty Officers' Mess, where Len worked, and out the other side, exploding twenty feet clear of the ship. Eighteen men were badly wounded and five died and were buried at sea. The *Athabaskan* limped home.

It was the second incident that resulted in the ship going down into the murky depths of the English Channel. In the early hours of April 29, 1944, two torpedoes from two different German boats hit the *Athabaskan* and the ship blew up in a massive explosion that could be seen from over twenty miles away. The crew were told to abandon ship. As the ship began to slide into its watery grave, Len had no choice but to jump into the oil-filled waters. A scant fifteen minutes later, the *Athabaskan* had slipped from sight and the captain and one hundred and twenty-eight of the crew were lost. Len spent what seemed like hours, swimming around in heavy oil, his water-soaked clothing weighing him down. Their sister ship, the HMCS *Haida*, was steaming toward them. When it came in sight, cries of "Go Haida" echoed across the water, but there was not enough time to rescue all of the survivors; eighty-three were picked up by German destroyers and taken as prisoners of war. Len was one of the forty-four who were fortunate enough to be rescued by the *Haida*.

By the time Len and Vie were married, he was working as a high-explosives expert and special dynamite engineer all over the province. Vie continued working as a food inspector until their daughter, Eileen, was born in 1952; then she quit work to stay home with their little girl. They wanted more children and when Eileen was three, Vie became pregnant again, this time with twin boys. The pregnancy went horribly wrong and Vie ended up with an ectopic pregnancy that nearly killed her.

"I was pregnant for the second time and partway through my first trimester I became quite ill. I was not one to run off to doctors but I knew something was not right. The doctor said to me, 'You are pregnant and all pregnant women feel unwell at some point in their pregnancy.' I tried to make it clear to him that what I was feeling was not normal and that I was really sick, but it seemed to fall on deaf ears. When doctors refuse to listen to you it's hopeless to try and explain anything more to them. In those days, you didn't push the issue. By that evening I was in a good deal of pain. I called the doctor again and explained the situation and he told me to get to the Abbotsford hospital immediately.

"I had no idea what was wrong, but by the time I got to the emergency ward I had lost a lot of blood and my blood pressure was dropping. The emergency room doctor told me I had a tubal pregnancy and that it was quite serious. He had never done the type of surgery I needed and no one else in the hospital had the experience to deal with it so they flew a team of surgeons in from Vancouver. I was fading in and out of consciousness and they didn't think I was going to make it. But sick as I was, I knew I had to pull through because I had this beautiful little daughter I loved so much who needed her mother to take care of her.

"When the team from Vancouver landed there was a car waiting to rush them to the hospital. They had me set up in the operating room and I vaguely remember a great big white light above me, probably the operating room light, and a group of doctors around me, talking in muted tones. I could barely make out what they were saying. Things were quite hazy; I really had no idea what was going on. I vaguely remember them telling me that until they could stop the hemorrhaging, I wouldn't be able to have a full anesthetic. All I said was, 'Do your thing, and whatever happens will happen.' That was the last thing I remembered."

As a highly specialized professional in explosives technology, Vie's husband worked in a high-risk industry, something she learned to live with. It was a stressful job that demanded clear, analytical thinking and a calm demeanor. Len was responsible for planning and executing the blasting, as well as the safety of the workers and the materials. It was also a job that required him to be away from home for long periods of time. In all their twenty-five years of marriage, they were together, at best, a total of six years. Vie, who was always independent, became even more so during her husband's absences. In the times he was away, she became the head of the house, though in the 1950s, propriety demanded that men assume the role as the dominant person. There was also the issue of child rearing. She was not really a single parent, but she had to take responsibility

You can't have too many shoes.

as if she were. It meant she had to be adaptable, taking control when her husband was gone and giving it back when he was home.

"Len was gone quite a lot all during the years of our marriage. Sometime in the late fifties he began working on Vancouver Island, so we moved there hoping that we could be together more. But it was still hard on all of us, our daughter included. It seemed that we would just get into a pattern and then have it disrupted when he had to go away again. It would take me a couple of weeks to get our daughter settled back into her daily regime and then we would start all over again when he came home. It was not the best situation, but what can you do?

"Len had a first-class job. It was challenging and demanding, and he was good at it. People in the industry said that he was one of the world's best blasters. He could blast a rock so clean that it looked like it had been cut with a knife. It was hazardous work and I always dreaded that a day might come when I received a knock on the door or a phone call to tell me that Len had been killed in a blasting accident."

One of the jobs that Vie's husband worked on, which received worldwide coverage, was the preparation for the blasting of Ripple Rock; it lay in Seymour Narrows, at the confluence of Discovery Passage and Johnstone Strait in BC's Inside Passage. Dangerous currents, tide rips, and swirling eddies funneled through a channel half a nautical mile in width. Ripple Rock, an underground mountain with two peaks that lay a mere ten feet under the surface of the water, was considered by seamen to be one of the worst hazards to marine navigation on the coast. It had claimed one hundred and fourteen lives and one hundred and twenty vessels over the years. On the morning of April 5, 1958, the twin tops were blown up in the largest commercial, non-nuclear explosion at the time. It had taken two and a half years of tunneling through the mountain to set the load and the resulting explosion spewed over six million tonnes of rock and water a thousand feet into the air.

Let the chips fall where they may **and don't worry. If you worry too much, you'll get old before your time.** That's what I would say.

"Len did some of the explosives work for Ripple Rock. He and another young man were working down about two hundred feet. After the day's work they decided to go for a cold beer. Harvey said that he wasn't feeling well. It turns out that he had the bends and they didn't have a hyperbaric chamber nearby. That poor lad ended up paralyzed for life.

"In the 1970s, Len was working for a company called Pat Carson Bulldozing on Vancouver Island. They had a job up in Green Cove on the Alberni Inlet near Bamfield. One of the forestry companies, MacMillan Bloedel, had contracted with Carson to do the blasting for a series of logging roads they were putting in. Len had to go pick up some of his crew in Port Alberni and bring them back to Green Cove. He and one of his co-workers were driving the company's crew cab along one of the newly developed logging roads. There were logging trucks coming and going all the time and the roads were only wide enough for one truck; there was no room for passing. The truckers all had radios to check each others' movements and location.

"I'll never forget the day. It was Tuesday, August 31, 1976, at ten in the morning. I got the phone call, the one that I never wanted to get. Len was outward-bound and there was a logging truck inbound. They both were coming around a mountain so neither one could see the other. The radio in the logging truck was not working that day; Len didn't know that. He was listening to hear if anything was coming but there was no communication so he would have assumed that the road was clear. Those logging trucks are huge and they drive at a pretty good clip. As they both came around the curve they met head-on. Len veered to miss the truck but it was too late. The shoulder on the roadbed was soft and couldn't support his truck. It went careening one hundred and fifty feet down the mountainside. When the rescuers got to him he was conscious. They asked him how he was doing and he said his head hurt. Those were the last words that my husband ever spoke. His co-worker, Glen Evans, was killed instantly. He was only twenty-one. He had his whole life before him, taken away in an instant.

"I was stunned. There are no words to explain how you feel at a time like that. Len was so young; he was only fifty-one. The hardest thing I have ever had to do was tell Eileen that her father had been killed in an accident. Breaking the news to her took a lot out of me. Life doesn't ever prepare you for that. How do you tell your child that her father has died? As a parent you try and protect your child and then something happens that takes that right out of your hands. You feel helpless.

"Intruding all too soon on our grief and sadness was the stark reality of my financial situation. Thank goodness I had a job but I didn't really earn enough to be self-supporting. I couldn't sue the company for compensation because in those days, your contractual agreements didn't allow for it. I hired a lawyer but he said there was nothing he could do: Len's contract tied his hands. I did receive ninety-eight dollars a month for a few years from Workmen's Compensation but even with my salary from work, it was not enough to live on. I really didn't know what to do. I was very frugal, my earlier background had taught me that, but thriftiness can only stretch a dollar so far. I lived in a small apartment and I got to thinking that I could rent out a couple of rooms, so I took in two boarders. We were packed in like sardines. It wasn't the best solution but for time being it was the only one."

AUNTIE VIE'S
Life After Len

Over the next sixteen years, Vie worked as a superintendent of two apartment buildings in Esquimalt, near Victoria, British Columbia. She took little time off. She did travel to Toronto to see her sister every once in a while, but in the main she worked hard, twenty-four hours a day, seven days a week. The job of managing the apartment buildings meant that she was unable to have much of a social life; she was on call around the clock. Her duties required her to take charge of the daily functioning and maintenance of both buildings, and the outside grounds as well. In a flower-loving city that is a lot of work, although it gave her a chance to plant the roses she had so loved as a child.

Vie's duties were quite varied and challenging, which suited her perfectly. She had to be conversant with the operation of all of the mechanical and technical systems; she was responsible for fire safety; and she had to discreetly and tactfully handle the renters' problems and concerns. Living in one of the apartments she managed, as was required, meant that there was never a division between her work and private space. It was also not the kind of job that someone else could do very well as a substitute. Vie certainly took advantage of her holidays but that did not make up for the long hours that she put in. Her job eventually took its toll and Vie ended up having a massive heart attack that she barely survived.

"I did everything. I buried people's beloved pets that had passed away; I managed the gardens and kept the walkways swept. If something wasn't working, like a garbage disposal, and I couldn't get a tradesman in to take care of it, I would fix it myself. I have had my head and hands down other people's toilets, up dryer vents, under sinks, and down drains. You name it and I've fixed it at one time or another. I got really good at multi-tasking. Sometimes it seemed like I could unclog a sink, change a light bulb, soothe ruffled feathers, and talk to a serviceman, all at the same time. I took care of the plumbing and the electrical systems, and I even had to monitor the steam boiler.

"That steam boiler was something else. There were pressure gauges, blow-off valves, automatic feeds—there were twenty-seven gauges and if you didn't watch every little dial to make sure each instrument was in the correct range, you could blow the whole building up in seconds.

As you get older, stay positive
and don't complain about your ailments.
I can't think of anything more depressing.

I remember at one point I had to call in a specialist to fix the boiler and I noticed that something had not been hooked up correctly. I said as much but he ignored me. Well, the door of the boiler blew off, swept past me and blew a hole in the side of the basement. I swear, I have a guardian angel that sits on my shoulder.

"It was hard work. I never got time to rest and I can't ever remember getting a full night's sleep. I would get a call in the middle of the night to fix something or other or to mediate between neighbors' quarrels—Number Twenty-Three complained that Number Twenty-Two had their television on too loud, but Number Twenty-Two said they couldn't hear very well and needed to turn it up—that sort of thing. You had to sort the problem out and always be diplomatic about it. It rattled your brain sometimes. By the time I got back to bed, I would be wide awake and couldn't sleep.

"Expect the unexpected, I always say. One early morning, I think it was around six o'clock, I was sweeping in back of one of the buildings. Out of nowhere, I had this crushing pain in my chest and, before I knew what had happened, I had collapsed in a heap on the ground. When I could, I crawled up the stairs to get to a phone and called my doctor. He sent an ambulance to pick me up. Later, in the hospital, my doctor said I had had a heart attack and was very lucky to be alive. Boy, I thought, 'God is not finished with me yet.' I now take so many darn pills I can hardly count them.

"There were many great times, though. I remember one very sweet little woman whose pet bird died. She was so upset. She asked if I could bury it for her. I tucked it very carefully into a small box that I lined with cotton. Then I took it out to the rose garden and dug a small hole for it and buried it. She asked me to sing 'Amazing Grace' over the grave. She couldn't come down but she was looking out the window of her apartment and she had tears streaming down her face. I looked up at her and my heart felt like it was going to burst. Sometimes a small pet like that is all people have left in the world, and if I could bring her comfort in any way I was more than happy to do it. Despite the hard work, I loved my clients and I'm still in touch with some of them even though I moved away a long time ago.

"I had quite a number of suitors after Len died. I didn't date much but I did go to dances with my niece or my daughter and son-in-law. I had stopped dancing when Len and I were married and I missed it. I went mostly to the Chief and Petty Officers' Mess at the Canadian Forces Base in Esquimalt. I loved going there. It's a beautiful place that sits right on the edge of the harbor. The view is spectacular. Deep-sea ships dot the horizon, there are seagulls gliding on the wind, boats of every description come and go, and in the distance the snow-capped Olympic Mountains tower over everything. Can you imagine dancing with that as a backdrop? The dances were formal and elegant, and I always enjoyed myself.

"I sometimes went to the Pro Patria Legion, which is a branch of the Royal Canadian Legion. The legion hall was also in Esquimalt. That was so much fun. It was more informal than the Chief and Petty Officers' Mess so it was a good balance. We danced mostly to country-and-western music. It felt good to get my toes tapping to that up-tempo beat again. It would bring me right back to my earlier barn-dancing days. There were other places for social dancing around the city but they weren't the kind of places where a single woman should go.

"You had to be careful. I always told the gentlemen I danced with that I didn't do the 'Home Sweet Home Waltz'; I was going home alone! I remember one 'gentleman' in particular. He was quite well off and he thought that he could use his wealth as a way to get me to marry him. I have never judged people on the amount of money they have or don't have and it has never influenced any of my decisions regarding my friendships. I don't think that was something he understood. He was also hopelessly possessive. He told me that he would take care of me for the rest of my life and that I would want for nothing but that when we were married, he didn't want me to see any of my relatives—not even my daughter—or my friends. He said that he was too jealous and that he wanted me all for himself. I told him that he had better run as fast as he could because if I caught him, I would do something to him that would change him from a rooster into a hen. I think he understood very clearly what I was saying. He disappeared and that was the end of him.

"I really had no desire to marry again. Men are a lot of hard work, at least they were in my generation. You had to do everything for them; they were like helpless babies. You cooked, you cleaned, you took care of your children, you worked full-time at a job and you got bossed around. Is it any different now? I wonder. I always say marriage is like a prison sentence: twenty-five to life. I have my daughter and my beautiful granddaughter, my large extended family, and my friends. They make my life worthwhile. I don't need a man to make me feel good about myself. That has to come from me, not from someone else. My dating days are way over but that doesn't mean I don't like to look. I may be eighty-five but I'm not in the ground yet. I like the John Wayne and Spencer Tracy type of men. They represented strong men who always knew how to treat a lady; they were polite and respectful and made you feel so elegant. Oh, and wearing a uniform doesn't hurt either. I do like a man in a uniform."

I am not going to resign **myself to getting old; I am still** going to wear pretty shoes.

After her heart attack, Vie had to leave her job. She was sixty-eight, too young to retire, she says. She needed to be quiet for a while and gather her strength. When she had the energy, she left her apartment in Esquimalt and moved, leaving a part of her behind. There were no role models to show her how to manage the next part of her life: a life without a job, without a timetable, empty of its former constant demands. Her identity had long been wrapped up in her working life and a sudden, unplanned-for change can stop a person for a moment. But rather than spend precious time pondering the metaphysics of it all, Vie seems to have been only temporarily winded. It was not long before she was up and reinventing her life.

Carol Anderson, Vie's niece, says that her aunt has a strong will to live. "That little lady has come out of so many emergencies so many times because she overdoes things. She doesn't know when to stop, especially when she gets dancing—she just loves life. She has such resolve and willpower. She never complains or mentions her health. She has such a strong spirit and is so resilient. I don't know what we would do without her. Auntie Vie is the person in our family that we all revolve around; she's the family matriarch."

Now, at eighty-five, Vie spends her time entertaining her relatives, cooking large family suppers, watching over her animals, giving cooking lessons to neighbors,

and responding to the many requests for media interviews and public appearances that her fame has brought. She overdoes it every once in a while and ends up in the hospital, but she has no time for contemplating life's ills or relaxing on her laurels. She is busy and energetic, and at this very moment is planning a class on pickling baby cucumbers. The jars are ready, a hundred cloves of garlic are peeled, the alum is bought, and the ham and potato salad for the students is in the fridge.

AUNTIE VIE'S THOUGHTS ON
fashion

Auntie Vie is something of a fashionista, although you will not find a piece of haute couture hanging in her closet. She is a thrifty shopper and looks for bargains but you do have to pay for design, she says. Her style is unique; she looks to the latest trends but has the ability to combine vintage clothing with modern fashion, and she is not afraid to be feminine.

"Enjoy being a woman," she instructs, "but to do that you don't have to be a slave to fashion; you would go broke very quickly if you were. Note the trends but adapt them to what you have. Buy classic, because a chic dress will never go out of style. You can always dress up a classic design with accessories." Auntie Vie has closets full of beautiful dresses and shoes, too many to count. "I was born to love clothes. Dresses, jewelry and shoes are my weakness. Perhaps it's because we didn't have such luxuries when we were growing up." Her fashion sense is part of her charm.

Shopping with Vie is quite an experience. Her niece Carol Anderson says, "I love shopping with Auntie Vie, although it can be exhausting—not for her but for me. She's so enthusiastic and she has a great sense of style. After a day of shopping, I want to go home and tuck all of my slacks away in a drawer and wear only beautiful dresses. She makes me feel feminine and young again."

When Auntie Vie was a young girl in rural Saskatchewan, there were no clothing stores or fashion centers nearby. People who lived far away from urban hubs could buy their clothing and shoes from the Eaton's catalog. Eaton's was the dominant mail-order business in the country but for Vie and her family, the catalog was a book of dreams only. Feeding a large family and keeping the farm going were far more important than buying dainty frocks. Vie's clothes were made of whatever material was around; most of them were hand-me-downs from her older sisters. "My sister Annie made our clothes. We had an old treadle sewing machine and she made us the prettiest clothes you ever did see. Sometimes we managed to get lace and she would trim our dresses with it so we would look nice for school."

> Look to the young **for fashion but adapt** the fashion for your age.

Much of the material for Vie's clothes came from flour sacks—a one-hundred-pound sack would yield about a yard of fabric. "Our flour came in beautiful gingham; green and white, red and white, and blue and white. I guess that's why gingham has often been thought of as farmers' material. I like gingham—I think it's fresh looking." Gingham has been in and out of fashion since the seventeenth century. Flour producers learned very quickly that women used their sacks for sewing projects so the companies competed with each other by regularly

Television interview with *Access Hollywood*. After filming, she fed the producer and crew her apple pie and pickles.

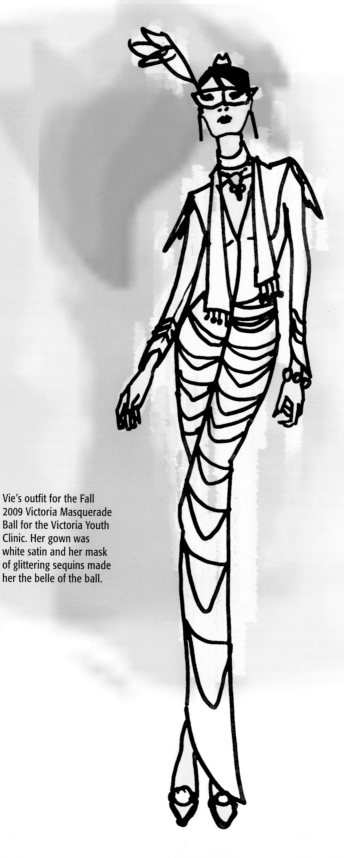

Vie's outfit for the Fall 2009 Victoria Masquerade Ball for the Victoria Youth Clinic. Her gown was white satin and her mask of glittering sequins made her the belle of the ball.

putting out new prints. People could often tell which kids belonged to a particular family by the style of print they were wearing.

Vie never had a ready-made dress until she was out working on her own. "I remember my first store-bought dress. It was after I received my very first paycheck. It was so exciting for me to look at all of the wonderful fashions in the shops, knowing that I could finally buy myself a real dress. There were so many beautiful choices. The fabrics were wonderful. There were dresses made of cotton, wool, silk, and tweed—all natural products. Synthetic fabrics were not yet manufactured; I don't think nylons came in until 1939. Most of women's skirts were mid-calf length and full below the hip. We wore fitted jackets and sweater sets with a single-strand pearl necklace. Women looked so feminine in those days.

"I remember that fur was popular as trim. It was used on our hats, our coat collars and sleeves, and our wraps and stoles. Even our hand muffs were made out of fur. The most popular trim was Alaskan sable (a fancy word for skunk), mink, and chinchilla. We had not yet reached the stage of awareness that we have today about the use of fur; at that time, no one gave it a thought. I hope we've learned a lot since then. My great-niece Pamela has worked very hard to bring awareness to all of us about the significance of ethical treatment for animals. What she is doing is awfully important and I am very proud of her.

Dress for yourself, but be chic about it.

"We all wore hats when we were out in public. Pillbox hats were popular, as were trimmed turbans and berets that we wore off to one side; they were very smart looking. Our shoes had rounded toes with thick, wide

Vie in Toronto in 1940—already
fashionable at sixteen.
FAMILY PHOTO

The peach-colored satin
gown Auntie Vie wore for
interviews with /A\ *News* and
eTalk during the grand finale
of *Dancing with the Stars*.

A favorite afternoon dress that Auntie Vie likes to wear for a luncheon or tea.

heels and our make-up tended toward the red tones to brighten our complexions.

"My very first dress was blue and had a wide belt and a flared skirt. A lot of dresses at the time were cut on the bias and they almost all had a seamed waistline covered by a belt. The sleeves were long and slightly puffed at the shoulder. It was very pretty. That dress was a milestone in my life. It represented my independence, my ability to take care of myself, and my growing sense of self-expression and self-determination. I had come a long way from my little gingham flour-sack dresses. When I think back, our poverty must have been hard for my mother. When she was little and living in Russia, my grandparents would have a tailor come to their house and live with them for a month, once a year. They had a room in their house specifically for him. During that month he would design, measure, cut and sew the clothing for the entire family. It's a stretch from having your own tailor to sewing clothes from flour sacks."

The hat designed for Auntie Vie by Philip Treacy.
ROLF HICKER PHOTOGRAPHY

PHILIP TREACY
LONDON

AUNTIE VIE'S hats

From an elegant little boutique in the heart of London's Belgravia district, a gentleman made a phone call on behalf of one of his friends. Vie was having her early-morning coffee when the phone rang and the voice at the other end said, "This is London, England, calling."

Vie had no idea who on Earth would be phoning her from London so she politely asked, "To what do I owe this pleasure?"

The voice at the other end said, "My name is Philip Treacy and your great-niece Pamela Anderson is here with me now and she would like to get you a hat."

Vie was stunned. Pamela often called her when she was away just to touch base but a phone call from Philip Treacy was completely unexpected. Philip Treacy is one of this century's foremost hat designers. He has designed hats for British royalty as well as the glitterati; Lady Gaga wore one of his designs for the 2009 Grammy awards and Sarah Jessica Parker wore one of his beautiful confections for the

UK premiere of *Sex and the City 2*. He has designed for Alexander McQueen's white Haute Couture collection for Givenchy in Paris and Karl Lagerfield at Chanel and he is an honorary Officer of the Most Excellent Order of the British Empire. His work is both avant-garde and elegant, and on Auntie Vie his hat transforms her from chic to diva.

"When the box came it looked like a refrigerator. It was so big. When I opened that box, there was another beautiful box inside. It was a deep royal blue and the lid had a gold unicorn embossed on it and underneath it read 'Philip Treacy London.' I ran my fingers over the letters; it looked so elegant. There were two hats. The first one was a lovely, smart-looking tam that brought me right back to the 1930s with a modern-day twist, and the second was a big red hat with plumes and roses that had jewel-encrusted stamens. The inside of the hat looks like a work of art all its own. I have never seen such magnificent hand-stitching. I can't even describe what I felt. I put the hat on and imagined I was the Queen. Here I am, an eighty-five-year-old woman dancing around in my kitchen with this beautiful hat on top of my head.

"When I was young, our English teacher took us to Saskatoon to see Queen Elizabeth and King George VI. I will never forget that visit. They were on a train and were only just stopping by for a wave and a quick appearance. I can always remember when they opened the train door and Their Majesties appeared. The Queen had a beautiful powder blue hat with big plumage, complimented by a blue dress. She had such a wonderful smile. She was so lovely, I thought. I loved her hat, and I just kept staring

Buy classics, because they **never go out of style. You may have to pay the price** but just have fewer clothes.

at it—I had never seen anything like that before. I would never have believed that one day I would be able to wear such a stunning hat. It just makes me feel good wearing it—like a queen."

Auntie Vie is frequently photographed in her gorgeous red hat with its side plumage and large silk flowers. It is the one item above all that the media insist on her wearing for her interviews. She has other hats but the red one is the one they all want; it has become her signature, part of her celebrity.

Her niece Carol says, "Auntie Vie would cook a chicken in her high heels."
ROLF HICKER PHOTOGRAPHY

AUNTIE
VIE

AUNTIE VIE'S
shoes

Auntie Vie loves shoes. She has dancing shoes, royal blue shoes with decorative trim, silver shoes, white satin shoes, clear shoes with rhinestone straps, red leather shoes with chic red bows, gold shoes, black patent leather shoes and pink satin bedroom heels with pompoms. She has forty pairs of shoes and counting. If she were younger she would probably have a closet full of Jimmy Choo shoes, too. What she does not have are boots, sensible shoes or runners. You will not find her walking in a shopping mall in sport shoes, sandals or laced-up granny shoes.

"You can't have too many shoes," she says. "I wonder how many more hundreds of pairs of shoes I'll get before I leave this world. I will say it is getting a little ridiculous, but—you only live once."

Vie spent her early life running around in bare feet or in wool felt shoes made by her mother. Shoes were available; you could buy them through the Eaton's catalog. They sold "milkmaid" shoes, a serviceable, lace-up shoe that was advertised for women who worked outdoors, and men could purchase sturdy work boots, but many farmers could not afford shoes at all for their children, regardless of style or the latest trend.

"We didn't wear shoes until the ground got really cold. Shoes were a luxury we couldn't afford. When there was frost on the ground, it got pretty darn cold on our feet. You learned to pick your feet up off the ground awfully fast; there was no lingering around chatting outdoors. For the winter months, Mother made us boots. We looked like the Beverly Hillbillies, I'll tell you. They had pointed toes and they laced up. Mother used to make our boots out of felt with rubber bottoms. The felt was good for dry snow and the rubber kept us dry when it was slushy. Mother would trim them with lace to make them look nicer for us.

"The first pair of store-bought shoes I ever owned was when I started working. They were black patent leather flats. I was fourteen. I bought them for my train trip when I went to work in the war plant in Ontario. I wore them with slacks and a nice blouse. They felt a bit strange at first, but I loved those shoes so much. I kept looking down at them to see how shiny they were. I didn't want to get one speck of dirt on them; I never wanted them to get old or wear out. They were perfect. I think I caught the shoe bug right then and there. My second pair was the steel-toed work boots that I had to wear at the munitions plant. They were heavy and clunky. I don't think you would use the word feminine to describe them! Functional, maybe—although they didn't protect me from the five-hundred-pound shell that was dropped on my foot. After my foot healed, I went shoe crazy."

Vie has thought a lot about shoes over the years and

I have different shoes **for each outfit.**

A few of her most recent additions.
ROLF HICKER PHOTOGRAPHY

has advice for those of us who may not give them much consideration. "I realize there are shoe people and those who are not particularly interested in their shoes. But I think some basic principles apply in buying shoes. It is important to buy fashionable shoes of good quality. They may cost a little more but if you buy quality shoes, they will hold their shape and their value. Take your time in choosing your shoes; they need to fit your feet. They have to be comfortable, and make sure they work with the outfit you intend to wear. Shoes can make or break an outfit. Too often you see people going out who have spent a lot of time with their hair and make-up and then you look down at their shoes and everything falls to pieces."

Her niece Carol confirms Auntie Vie's passion for beautiful shoes. "When most of us go shopping we look at sensible shoes, especially as we get older, but then you go shopping with this eighty-five-year-old lady and she buys dainty shoes and slingbacks. She even puts beautiful shoes on to cook a chicken."

"I do have a lot of slingback shoes," Vie says. "They're so handy; you can wear them for all kinds of occasions. They look good with a nice pair of slacks and they can be worn with evening attire, too. They don't have to be high, but a slight heel lengthens your leg and makes your ankle look slender. They are particularly good for shorter women like me. If you're having trouble walking and you can't wear heels, then dress the shoe up with some nice detail, like beading or bows. It will add a bit of flair to the shoes. Put some spring in your step and some glitz in your life—that's what I say. Don't forget to wear stockings. Even if you have beautiful legs, stockings make them look better."

AUNTIE
VIE

AUNTIE VIE ON
dancing

Auntie Vie was born to dance and has the legs to do it, although since she has a serious heart condition, her dances are a little shorter and her steps a little smaller than they once were. "I have always danced," she says. "When the day comes that I have to leave this earth, I'll strap on my dancing shoes and waltz my way to the heavens. Just look up at the stars because I'll be lighting each one of them with a tap from my toe."

The most glamorous time for dancing, according to Vie, was in the 1930s and '40s during the era of the Big Bands, when dance palaces like Casa Loma in Toronto, the Hollywood Palladium in Los Angeles, the Savoy in New York—touted as the world's most beautiful ballroom—and the Chateau Laurier in Ottawa were fashionable. There were also dance halls scattered in small communities; boats hired dance bands for evening cruises on lakes; and fancy hotels had their own orchestras and offered social dance evenings and masked balls. If you didn't have a partner, that was no problem; you could visit one of the many taxi-dance halls where you could find the dime-a-dance girls and swing or jive until your money ran out. People were dance crazed; if there was music, they would dance.

Dancing studios and academies sprang up all over the place; the Arthur Murray dance studios were particularly popular. People roller-skated and ice-skated to Big Band music but the dance palaces held particular appeal; they were elegant and very elaborate with ornate décor, velvet draperies, and star casts of musicians. Dancers waltzed to the music of Guy Lombardo and his Royal Canadians, Benny Goodman, and Duke Ellington, and stars like singer Frank Sinatra and trumpeter Tommy Dorsey traveled to dance palaces across North America. But as the 1950s rolled in, Big Band music and the dance palaces faded into distant memory. Rock 'n' roll and television, as a new medium of entertainment, took their place. Television created the wildly popular *American Bandstand*, which taped teens bopping, bunnyhopping, doing the twist, and jiving. There have been periodic nostalgic fads for Big Band music and formal dancing but after the initial enthusiasm, it drops back into obscurity.

More recently, however, television has begun to marry people's ever-present passion for music and dancing with a significant revival in ballroom dance. In 2005, a reality television show, a spinoff of the British *Strictly Come Dancing* series, made its quiet debut in North America. It was called *Dancing with the Stars* and its chances of survival were not particularly good, given that it dealt with

Dance! If you can't dance, **just watch people dance and if you can't watch, then listen to dance music,** and if you can't listen, then imagine— it will keep you young.

formal ballroom dancing. But viewers loved watching and dreamily imagined fox trotting and waltzing across the dance floor with the contestants; they couldn't get enough of the sultry tango, the hip-rocking mambo and the energetic lindy hop. The program became a sensation; *Dancing with the Stars* has been franchised to more than thirty countries and has received four consecutive Emmy Awards in the United States.

The program pairs professional dancers with actors, football players, Olympic athletes, musicians, teenage heartthrobs, and the occasional astronaut. At the end of each performance, the public can phone in to vote for their favorite star. The popularity of *Dancing with the Stars* has spawned similar programs, such as *So You Think You Can Dance* and *Skating with Celebrities*.

The dress that Auntie Vie wore to a family wedding.

There are now DVDs featuring ballroom dancing for cardiovascular workouts, for weight loss and for body toning, and books on social dancing, too many to mention. Dance studios have waitlists and there are hundreds of YouTube videos with instructions on every type of ballroom dance. This revival appears to have staying power, as eager parents rush to register their tots for professional dancing classes.

Auntie Vie and her great-niece Pamela Anderson represent the solidifying of two great eras of dance and dance revival. Pamela's appearance on *Dancing with the Stars* allowed her to bridge seventy years, step into her great-auntie's shoes and dance the steps of classical ballroom dancing the way Vie did when she was younger.

"As youngsters, we were always dancing. Whether it was hard stomping to country-and-western music surrounded by our cows and horses in a barn dance or gliding across a beautiful wooden floor in a full-length lamé gown, I danced. When I worked in Toronto I went to every dance there was. My favorite place was Casa Loma, the house on the hill. My sister and I would go to Casa Loma for ballroom dancing.

"It still exists today—a beautiful, medieval-looking castle with towers and turrets; a great hall with sixty-foot ceilings; high, arched, leaded-glass

Don't ever wear dowdy clothes. **You will not only be depressed but you will be depressing to others.** Never give up on how you look.

windows; and secret passageways. It looks like Camelot: you could almost see knights in their shining armor riding up to the front. Casa Loma was originally owned by a wealthy Toronto financier, Sir Henry Pellatt, who built it as a home for himself and his family. During the war it had been used as a bomb shelter for Toronto's important VIPs, probably because it had a series of tunnels eighteen feet under the castle. It used to be fun to explore those tunnels. Casa Loma was the place to be and was at the center of Big Band music.

"The dances were very formal; the men wore suits and the women wore formal ball gowns. It was perfect, because it not only fueled my passion for dancing but it gave me the opportunity to wear beautiful dresses. I remember a gorgeous pink taffeta ballroom gown I bought. It had a lovely flared skirt that moved so gracefully when I waltzed. I wore pearl earrings and had white satin heels. The dance floor was beautiful. It was wood, of course; it was so inviting. I don't know if it was a sprung floor but it felt like a proper dance floor to me. It was easy to glide across and was perfect for pivoting on the toe of your shoe. We danced to a live orchestra that played Big Band music. The men in the orchestra wore handsome suits with black bow ties and black satin lapels. They played on a dais that was framed by a towering window that had full, heavy velvet curtains on either side. The music was sweet and romantic and the ballroom was bathed in blue light. I would float around the floor feeling like I was dancing under a moonlit night. We danced to Frank Sinatra, Bing Crosby, Lawrence Welk; all of the big names came to Casa Loma.

"We learned to do all of the dances at the time, although they were mainly different types of waltzes; the samba, jive, and lindy hop came later. I could lose five pound a night dancing. I never stopped. When we couldn't go to Casa Loma, we would go roller-skating and skate-dance to Big Band music. Roller dance was

You can lose five pounds **a night by just dancing.** Join clubs and dance.

Hi Auntie Vie,

So did you like my comment on Larry King about my sexy Aunt?!

You have always been an inspiration to me. Your spirit has always been fun. You've been true to yourself.

I think some of my outfits on V.I.P. were right out of your closet!

Stay well, stay happy and keep dancing.

I'll see you very soon.
Pamela

A letter from Pamela to her Auntie Vie after an interview on *Larry King Live* on April 14, 2010, in reference to Pamela's appearance on *Dancing with the Stars*.

very popular during the 1930s and '40s; everybody went. We skated to waltzes, marches, and the tango. It was like ballroom dancing but on roller skates. It was so much fun. I loved watching my great-niece on *Dancing with the Stars*. It brought back so many memories of my dancing days."

AUNTIE VIE'S
kitchen

The kitchen is the first room you enter when you come into Auntie Vie's house; it is the heart of her home. Although she has a lovely dining room for formal occasions, the kitchen is where her guests and family gather for a cup of coffee, a chat, and a slice of one of her delicious pies. Her kitchen is a great leveler and everyone, no matter who, always gets the special Auntie Vie treatment. If a camera crew arranges to interview her in the morning or family members call to say they are coming for a visit, she will get up early to make a fresh pie or have a plate of hors d'oeuvres waiting. Her kitchen is the place where she responds to the many calls from the media; it is where she greeted Philip Treacy when he called from England about the hat he was designing for her; it is where she dances; and it is the place from which dozens of jars of pickled dills, watermelon pickles, preserves, and sweet honey mustard, as well as soups, perogies, roasts, pies, and cakes emerge.

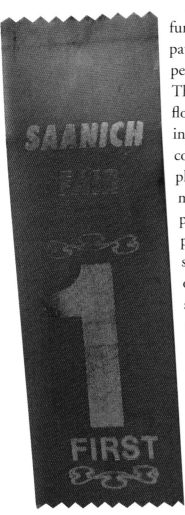

One of Auntie Vie's many first-place ribbons for her pickles and mustard.

Auntie Vie's kitchen is an inviting, cozy room furnished with white cabinets, black-and-white patterned flooring, pale pink valences and a table perpetually set with freshly ironed white linen. There are always vases of tastefully arranged flowers that complement the delectable cooking aromas emanating from the oven. In the corner by the phone, a radio/compact disc player hums waltzes, tangos, and Hawaiian music. Her refrigerator is decorated with family photos and memorabilia. There are numerous pictures of her granddaughter winning ice-skating competitions, a snapshot of several of Vie's culinary delights, and a photo of her son-in-law's award-winning sand sculpture, taken at an international competition. There are pictures of Pamela, arms loaded with jars of her great-auntie's pickles and a few of Vie dancing with various television producers and program hosts. At the bottom of the fridge, almost out of eyesight, there is a tidy arrangement of Vie's blue ribbons, won for her dills, mustards, and pies. It is a delightful mixture of keepsakes that speaks to her love of people, the important place of family in her life and her culinary expertise.

On the wall next to the table, and above a photo of her father and mother, hangs a watercolor that stirs childhood memories of cold winter days on the prairies, crunching white snow, and sweet scents of cooking escaping the house on a whiff of wind, greeting those who came near. "Mother had a beautiful wood-burning chrome stove in her kitchen, the kind that had a warming oven on the top. She always had something cooking on it but she kept it spotless. It was big; it took up a large part of the kitchen. I think it was about six feet long. She would bake six loaves of fresh bread three to four times a week—she used a hundred pounds of flour a week. When we came home from school we could smell the bread baking half a mile away. You could almost taste it, it smelled so good. People were always asking to buy her bread but she said no to all requests because, she told them, she already had a large family to cook for and she simply did not have the time to bake extra loaves.

"Mother was such a good cook. We always had nice food. Her perogies were delicious. She would fry bacon and eggs to serve with them—we loved those meals. She baked the most beautiful cakes. Just thinking about it makes my mouth water. There were no stores nearby and the winters were harsh, so we had to provide for ourselves. We had our own milk from our cows, eggs from our chickens, and lard from butchering our pigs. We had turkeys and geese, too. Sometimes we would have thirty-seven people around the table and mother would cook a goose, a ham, and a turkey with all of the trimmings, and we would dig in."

What good are all the accolades **in life if you don't have** friends to enjoy them with?

Vie didn't learn to cook on that big stove; in fact, she really didn't learn to cook from her mother at all. She did, however, have a good grounding in wholesome food, and her mother's cooking left her with a discriminating palate. "I left home when I was just fourteen, so I never had the opportunity to learn to cook. I basically learned to cook out of necessity; it was either cook or starve. There was no packaged food in those days, but even if there had been I wouldn't have bought it. You never know what's in that stuff."

Auntie Vie often cooks with her most important help by her side: her granddaughter, Amy.
ROLF HICKER PHOTOGRAPHY

When she married, Vie cooked non-stop, sometimes to excess. Her husband had been brought up on a big farm in Saskatchewan and was used to hearty meals. "Honest to god," she says, "it was hard enough doing a turkey, but then to do a great big goose and a ham for the same meal—it was enough to make you weep." It could have turned her against cooking, but it didn't. Delicious meals are still coming out of her kitchen; good food is in her blood. Her Mennonite cooking roots run deep. "My motto," she says, "is good food makes for happy people."

Auntie Vie cooks from years of experience. She instinctively knows the right amounts and the proper look of a mixture: a teacup of this, a pinch of that, not too hot, not hot enough, the mixture should coat the spoon, kind of thick, not too thin, the texture has to be rich and soft, boil for ten minutes, maybe a bit less, it depends . . . She does not use a recipe, at least not one that is written down.

You need to be watchful when you're following her instructions because she is quick. For the purposes of the recipes included in this book, we have tried to standardize the measurements. Vie still uses teacups, pinches, and dashes but, in most cases, the various teacups were counted and then matched with a measuring cup. Periodically, her frustration with the tediousness of precise measuring would grow and, out of nowhere, a large dollop of flour would come flowing out of the bag and into the mixture. "It needs to be thickened up," she would say. Consequently, the recipes in this book are written with many approximations.

"It doesn't matter," Vie says. "Experiment and have fun. Follow your intuition—a good cook always knows." For the rest of us, a little patience and practice will yield wonderful results.

Cooking perogies for the camera crew.
ROLF HICKER PHOTOGRAPHY

AUNTIE VIE'S
favorite
recipes

Deep Dish Apple Pie

ROLF HICKER PHOTOGRAPHY

Pastry

2 cups (500 mL) pastry or all-purpose flour

½ tsp (2 mL) salt

¾ cup (185 mL) Crisco shortening,
cut into small pieces and chilled

4 Tbsp (60 mL) chilled water

Filling

8 to 10 tart green apples,
Granny Smith variety or similar

¾ cup (185 mL) sugar

2 tsp (10 mL) cinnamon

1 Tbsp (15 mL) all-purpose flour

I like my pie served at room temperature with a generous portion of
freshly made whipped cream, or
vanilla ice cream. The trick to making
a flaky pastry is keeping the Crisco
cold so cut the shortening into small
pieces and chill them in a bowl in
the refrigerator.

In a large bowl, combine the flour and salt, and then add the chilled shortening. Blend in the shortening with a pastry cutter or your fingers until the mixture resembles coarse flakes, like oatmeal.

Add the chilled water, a bit at a time, until the pastry sticks together. If the dough is too sticky, add a bit more flour. Turn the dough out onto a floured counter and knead lightly two or three times, and then form the mixture into a ball or a disc. Don't overwork the dough or your pastry will be tough.

Separate the dough into two balls, place on a plate or in a bowl and cover with a tea towel, then put them in the refrigerator to rest for about 30 minutes. In the meantime, preheat the oven to 350°F (180°C) and prepare the filling.

Peel, core, and slice the apples into thin pieces, and add them to a large bowl. Combine the sugar, cinnamon, and flour in a small bowl, and then sprinkle overtop the apple slices, tossing gently to coat well.

Remove the pastry from the refrigerator and roll out each ball on a lightly floured board until about ⅛ inch (3 mm) thick and 13 inches (33 cm) in diameter. Roll the dough starting from the center of the pastry, turning it a bit at a time. Make sure you don't roll over the edges or you will end up with a pie shell that splits at the edges and goes off in all directions.

Line a 9- or 10-inch (23- or 25-cm) pie plate with the one of the pastry rounds, gently pressing the pastry into the edges of the plate. You don't want to stretch the dough or it will shrink in the oven.

(If you want, you can seal the bottom of the pastry with a light wash of egg white using a pastry brush.)

Fill the pie shell with the apple mixture, heaping some of the apples into the center of the pie. This will give a nice rise to your pie as the apples shrink while baking—your food not only has to taste good but it needs to be presented attractively. Cover the apples with the other pastry round. Trim both edges to within about a ½ inch (1.25 cm) of the pie plate's rim and press them together using your fingers or a fork.

Make a few slits in the top of the pie with a knife to allow steam to escape. (I don't usually coat the top crust with an egg or milk wash, but you can if you want.) Cover the pie loosely with a piece of aluminum foil to keep the pastry from burning; you may also want to put a pan under the pie plate to catch any of the juice that leaks from the pie.

Place the pie in the middle of your preheated oven and bake for about 45 to 60 minutes. After 30 to 40 minutes, remove the aluminum foil and continue baking until the pie is done.

Makes 1 pie.

Lemon Pie with Graham Cracker Crust

Crust

1½ cups (375 mL) graham cracker crumbs

1 Tbsp (15 mL) fine sugar, to taste

4 Tbsp (60 mL) unsalted butter

Filling

¾ cups (185 mL) sugar

2 egg yolks

4 Tbsp (60 mL) cornstarch

Zest from 1 lemon

½ cup (125 mL) freshly squeezed lemon juice

2 cups (500 mL) boiling water

Making lemon pie may seem a bit fussy, but once you dip your spoon in the pot and savor the lemony tang of the pudding filling, you will never buy a pre-made lemon pie again.

In a medium-sized bowl, mix the graham cracker crumbs with sugar.

For the next step, you want to brown the butter, which will give the crust a nice, nutty taste. Put the butter in a saucepan and cook on medium heat. When the butter begins to foam, reduce the heat slightly. Continue cooking until the butter turns a nice caramel color. Don't overcook; a few seconds too long and the butter will burn. Take the browned butter off the stove and pour immediately overtop the graham cracker mix. Stir until blended.

Transfer the mixture to a 9- or 10-inch (23- or 25-cm) pie plate. Using a fork or your fingers, gently press the mixture into the bottom and sides of the pie plate. Chill for about 1 hour while you prepare the filling. Note: I don't bake my crust prior to filling because it already has a nutty taste from the browned butter. It does come out a bit more crumbly but I prefer it that way.

In a large bowl, beat the egg yolks for a few seconds with a whisk or an electric beater, just enough to blend them together. Add the sugar and beat for about 2 to 3 minutes, until lemony yellow and thick—about the same consistency as tub margarine. Add the cornstarch and mix until there are no lumps. Next, stir in the lemon zest and then add the lemon juice, pouring in a bit at a time. Mix until blended.

Using a wooden spoon, stir continuously while slowly adding the boiling water to the pudding, dribbling it in a thin stream. This part is tricky: add the boiling water too quickly and the eggs will curdle.

Transfer the mixture to a heavy saucepan and cook the pudding on medium heat, stirring continuously, until it thickens. You will know it is done when the temperature reaches 180°F (82°C) on a candy thermometer, or when it leaves a coating on the spoon. (Run a finger across the coated spoon and if the filling doesn't run, it is done.) Be careful not to overcook or it will liquify. Note: The filling will continue to thicken as it cools.

Transfer the filling to a bowl and cover with a plate to prevent a filmy layer from forming as it cools. (Don't use plastic wrap as a cover because the filling will continue to cook.)

When cooled, pour the filling into the chilled graham cracker crust. If you want, you can put the pie in the refrigerator to set, but I like mine at room temperature. And in my house it never lasts long enough to make it into the refrigerator.

Makes 1 pie.

Dark Chocolate Cake with Frosting

Cake

2 cups (500 mL) cake and pastry flour

2 tsp (10 mL) baking powder

1 tsp (5 mL) baking soda

¾ cup (185 mL) unsalted butter

3.5 oz (100 g) good-quality, semi-sweet dark chocolate (I use 2 bars of Hershey's Special Dark Chocolate)

3 eggs, at room temperature

¾ cup (185 mL) fine white sugar

1 cup (250 mL) cocoa powder

2 tsp (10 mL) pure vanilla

2 Tbsp (30 mL) dark rum

1 cup (250 mL) sour cream

½ cup (125 mL) semi-sweet chocolate chips

2⅓ cups (580 mL) table cream

Frosting

½ cup (125 mL) unsalted butter

¾ cup (185 mL) cream cheese

1½ cups (375 mL) icing sugar

2 tsp (10 mL) vanilla

2 Tbsp (30 mL) table cream

Dried shredded coconut, for topping

This is a very rich cake. Don't use diet anything for this recipe: you want full-fat sour cream, butter, and table cream. This is a treat so you probably won't make it often, but when you do, throw away your calorie counter.

Preheat the oven to 350°F (180°C). Grease and lightly flour a 9-inch (23-cm) Bundt cake pan, making sure you get into all the nooks and crannies. Set aside.

Sift together the flour, baking powder, and baking soda. Do this two times, and then set aside.

Melt the butter in a saucepan and set aside. Using a double boiler, melt the chocolate, stirring continuously. (If you don't have a double boiler, set a small saucepan over a larger one.)

Take the melted chocolate off the heat and add in the melted butter, stirring rapidly until the mixture is smooth. Set aside to cool slightly.

In a large bowl, beat the eggs and sugar together until the mixture is fluffy and has turned a pale yellow. Add the butter–chocolate mixture and stir until blended. Mix in the cocoa powder, vanilla, rum, and sour cream. Taste for sweetness before adding any sugar and then add just enough. (You don't want to add too much sugar because it will make the cake tough.) Add the flour mixture and stir.

Before folding in the chocolate chips, coat them lightly with a small amount of flour, which will keep them from sinking to the bottom of the cake.

Add the cream, a bit at a time. You don't want the mixture to be too thick nor too thin: when you lift your spoon, you want the batter to fold in on itself, and have the consistency of ketchup.

Pour the batter into the prepared pan and bake in the middle of the oven for about 45 minutes, or until a cake tester comes out clean. Insert your tester into the middle of the cake, not at the sides, since cakes cook from the sides inward. Cakes can be finicky and if you open the oven door too soon the cake will not cook properly and will likely fall.

When done, take the cake out of the oven and let it cool for 10 minutes. It seems to be the magic number—less than that and the cake will break into pieces; any longer and it may stick to the sides of the pan.

Remove the cake from the pan and place on a wire rack until completely cooled. While the cake cools, prepare the frosting.

In a medium-sized bowl, mix together the first five frosting ingredients until smooth, and then spread over the cooled cake with a spatula. Sprinkle coconut over the top and sides.

Makes 1 frosted cake.

Bailey's Irish Cream Coconut Bread Pudding with Irish Cream Custard Sauce

1 loaf unsliced white bread

2 cups (500 mL) mixed dried fruit like raisins, apricots, and prunes, diced

1 Tbsp (15 mL) all-purpose flour

¼ to ½ cup (60 to 125 mL) unsalted butter

6 eggs

14 oz (398 mL) can coconut milk

⅔ cup (80 mL) sweetened condensed milk

1 cup (250 mL) table cream

½ cup (125 mL) Bailey's Irish Cream

2 tsp (10 mL) vanilla

Small handful shredded unsweetened coconut

Bread pudding was a staple in my house growing up because it helped use up any leftover bread. We also we had our own chickens and cows so we had plenty of eggs and milk. This particular recipe is not the typical version I ate growing up—ours was less exotic. I know when we talk about food we often refer back to our grandmother's cooking, but this is definitely not my grandmother's bread pudding! It's a recipe that I have experimented with over the years and I still tweak it once in a while.

Preheat the oven to 350°F (180°C) and grease a 9 × 12 (3.5 L) pan.

Cut the crusts off the bread, slice into about 12 slices, and then cut into cubes. Place the bread in a large bowl. Melt the butter and lightly coat the bread with it. Set aside.

Place the dried fruit in another bowl, and sprinkle with just enough flour to coat it, which will help keep it from sinking to the bottom of the pudding. Add the flour-coated fruit to the bread and mix well.

In a separate bowl, whisk the eggs until frothy, and then add the coconut milk, condensed milk, cream, Bailey's Irish Cream, vanilla, and dried coconut. Stir until well blended. Pour over the bread and fruit mixture and gently blend together with a fork. You want enough liquid for the bread to look sort of soupy but not too much. Don't let it sit for long as the bread can soak up all of the liquid and dry out.

Spoon the bread pudding into the prepared pan, cover with aluminum foil, and bake for about 1 hour, or until a toothpick comes out clean. After 40 minutes, remove the foil so the top will brown. If the top is not browned enough after 1 hour, stick it under a low broiler for a few minutes.

Serves 8 to 10.

Serve warm with Bailey's Irish Cream Custard Sauce.

Irish Cream Custard Sauce

4 egg yolks, at room temperature

3 Tbsp (45 mL) fine granulated sugar

⅓ cup (80 mL) Bailey's Irish Cream

2 tsp (10 mL) cornstarch

2 cups (500 mL) cream, at room temperature

In a medium bowl, mix together the egg yolks, sugar, and Bailey's Irish Cream; set aside. In another bowl, mix the cornstarch with just enough water until it dissolves and no lumps remain; set aside.

Using a heavy saucepan, heat the cream on low until scalded, which is just below the boiling point—you will see small bubbles appear around the edge of the pan. Temper the egg mixture with the hot cream by slowly pouring half of the warmed cream into the eggs while stirring continuously. Doing so will bring the egg mixture up to the temperature of the cream. Pour the egg mixture back into the saucepan you used to heat the cream and stir continuously. Consulting a candy thermometer, mix in the liquified cornstarch once the temperature reaches 160°F (71°C). Keep stirring until the mixture thickens, at about 170°F (77°C). Do not overcook since custard curdles at 180°F (82°C). After the sauce is ready, it is a good idea to strain it to filter out any bits of egg yolk that may have become lumpy. Set aside and let cool for 5 to 10 minutes. Place cooled custard sauce in a bowl and cover with a plate to prevent a thin crust from forming on the top.

Jars of delicious honey mustard.

Pickles and pearls.
ROLF HICKER PHOTOGRAPHY

Coconut Prawns with Dipping Sauce

Prawns

10 jumbo prawns

2 Tbsp (30 mL) cornstarch

4 Tbsp (60 mL) white vinegar

Batter

½ cup (125 mL) cornstarch

½ cup (125 mL) all-purpose flour

½ cup (125 mL) finely shredded,
unsweetened coconut

2 Tbsp (30 mL) sesame seeds

Canola oil, safflower oil, or lard, for frying

Dipping Sauce

½ cup (125 mL) chili sauce

2 tsp (10 mL) medium-hot creamed horseradish

In a small bowl, mix the chili sauce with
the horseradish.

The secret to a light, greaseless prawn is the cornstarch. You can eat my prawns with white gloves and not get any grease on them.

Peel and de-vein the prawns, leaving the tails on. (To de-vein prawns, take a small, sharp knife and cut along the black line on the back of the prawn and remove it.) Next, butterfly each prawn by making a deep cut—about three-quarters of the way through—the length of the back to the tail. Rinse prawns in cold water.

Mix the cornstarch and vinegar together in a medium-sized bowl and soak the prawns in it while you prepare the batter.

In a medium-sized bowl, mix together the cornstarch, flour, coconut, and sesame seeds. Add the soaked prawns and stir to coat evenly. Set aside.

In a deep fryer or large, deep saucepan, heat the oil or melt the lard until the temperature reaches about 375°F (180°C); you will end up with greasy prawns if you fry them at a lower temperature. (If you don't have a thermometer, you can easily test its readiness by dipping a wooden spoon into the hot oil—when it sizzles around the spoon, it's hot enough to cook the prawns.) Being careful of spattering hot oil, fry the prawns 5 at a time until they turn a beautiful, crispy golden-brown. Remove them from the oil and place on paper towels to drain.

Serves 2.

Deep-Fried Chicken Wings

16 to 18 uncooked chicken wings
(a large family pack)

2 garlic cloves, peeled

1 cooking onion, peeled

Coating

½ cup (125 mL) cornstarch

½ cup (125 mL) dried breadcrumbs

1 tsp (5 mL) salt

1 tsp (5 mL) pepper

1 tsp (5 mL) paprika

1 tsp (5 mL) poultry seasoning

1 tsp (5 mL) ground ginger

1 tsp (5 mL) garlic powder (not garlic salt)

½ tsp (5 mL) dried mustard powder

Canola oil, safflower oil, or lard, for frying

I never seem to make enough of these wings. My family is always disappointed when the last chicken wing is eaten. You can eat these wings dressed for a ball. You will not get any oil on your outfit or end up with greasy fingers.

Bring a pot of water to boil, and then add the chicken wings, garlic, and onion. Bring the water to boiling again and continue cooking for 10 to 15 minutes. Remove the chicken wings with a slotted spoon and set aside to drain. Discard the garlic and onion.

Mix all of the coating ingredients together in a bag and then add the drained chicken wings. Shake it up to ensure a nice even coating.

In a deep fryer or large, deep saucepan, heat the oil or melt the lard until the temperature reaches about 375°F (180°C); you will end up with greasy chicken if you fry the wings at a lower temperature. Deep-fry the coated chicken until crispy-crunchy and golden-brown. Be sure not to crowd the chicken in the pan, as doing so will cause the temperature to drop. Fry for about 8 to 10 minutes, turning over once. You can tell if the chicken is cooked by cutting into a thick piece of the meat; if the juice is no longer pink, it's done. Remove from the pan and place on paper towels to drain.

Makes 16 to 18 wings.

Cottage Cheese Perogies with Gravy and Rhubarb Sauce

Gravy

1 cooking onion, diced

Unsalted butter, for sautéing

2 Farmer's sausages,
or 1 lb (500 g) smoked ham

3 cups (750 mL) sour cream

1 cup (250 mL) evaporated milk

Dough

2 egg whites, at room temperature
(save the yolks for the filling)

2 cups (500 mL) whipping cream

Dash of salt

4 cups (1 L) all-purpose flour

Filling

2⅓ cups (580 mL) dry-curd cottage
cheese (sometimes known as Farmer's
cheese or baker's cheese)

2 egg yolks (saved from making the dough)

Dash of pepper

My mother used to make these perogies for all 10 of us; it was a big job but we always eagerly awaited that first bite when they came out of the pot and right onto our plates. I once made 300 perogies for a big family reunion—that was a two-day marathon.

There are two things you should know before making perogies. The first is to forget about your diet and your cholesterol. For instance, don't be tempted to substitute milk for the whipping cream in the dough. Do that and it will be tough; use whipping cream to make a lovely, rich dough. The second is to ignore the state of your kitchen during the process. By the time you finish making this recipe, you will have a fine dusting of flour on your kitchen cabinets, stove, and floor. Eat these perogies hot out of the pan and worry about the kitchen later.

Finally, when buying Farmer's sausages, be sure to get quality ones, even though they can be hard to find. Farmer's sausage is a smoked pork sausage that has its roots in Mennonite cooking. We used to make our own sausages on the farm when I was little. We had a smokehouse and my mother would hang links of sausages over a rack to smoke them.

In a cast-iron frying pan, sauté the onion in a small bit of butter until it turns golden yellow, about 5 to 7 minutes. Remove from the pan and set aside.

Slice the sausages in half lengthwise, or cut the ham into medium-thick slices, and fry the meat in the same frying pan you used to cook the onions. When the meat is cooked to a lovely golden-brown color, remove from the pan and set aside for serving later with the perogies.

Leave the drippings in the pan and add the sour cream, evaporated milk, and sautéed onions. Stir continuously on medium-low heat until the mixture thickens, about 10 to 15 minutes. Take the pan off the stove and set aside while you prepare the dough and filling.

In a large bowl, mix the egg whites and whipping cream until blended. (I use a stainless steel whisk.)

Add the salt, and then mix in the flour, about 2 cups at a time, until the dough can be kneaded without sticking to your hands. You may need more or less than 4 cups (1 L) flour. The dough should feel light and soft.

Turn it out onto a floured countertop and knead until it is smooth and can be molded into a ball. Be careful not to overwork the dough. Cover with a tea towel and let it rest while you make the filling.

Mix the cottage cheese, egg yolks, and pepper in a bowl and set aside.

Pinch off a handful of dough and keep the rest covered with a tea towel to prevent it from drying out.

Lifting the dough and turning it as you go, roll out the dough until it is about ⅛ inch (3 mm) thick. Cut a 3½-inch (9-cm) wide circle using an upturned teacup or biscuit cutter.

Place a heaping tablespoon (15 mL) of filling into the center and fold the dough in half to create a half-moon shape. Pinch the edges together with your fingers. (If they don't stick together, your dough may be too dry. In that case, moisten the edge with a drop of egg white to get a good seal.) The important thing is to ensure there are no holes in any of the perogies, otherwise the filling will bleed through during cooking and you will have a cloudy, gummy mess in your cooking pot.

Repeat until you have used up all the dough. As you finish each perogy, rest it on a floured cookie sheet.

When you are ready to cook the perogies, bring a large pot of water to boiling and add some filled perogies. (Don't crowd the pot.) Bring the water back to boiling and cook the perogies until they float to the surface, and then cook for 4 more minutes. (The entire process takes about 8 to 10 minutes.) Using a slotted spoon, remove them from the pot, drain them in a colander, and then lay them on a buttered cookie sheet. Repeat the process until all of the perogies have been cooked.

To serve, place cooked perogies on each plate, spoon gravy overtop, and add some Farmer's sausage or ham slices on the side. Serve with rhubarb sauce.

Makes 2 to 3 dozen.

Rhubarb Sauce

A serving of rhubarb sauce on the side makes a nice addition to the perogies. When choosing rhubarb, buy strawberry or dark-red rhubarb; the lighter-colored rhubarb becomes stringy when cooked.

6 cups (1.5 L) fresh rhubarb, chopped into 1-inch (2.5 cm) pieces
1 cup (250 mL) sugar, to taste
6 Tbsp (90 mL) water

Add all the ingredients to a stainless steel or enameled pot. Cook on medium-high heat, stirring continuously, until the sugar dissolves.

Reduce the heat to medium-low and simmer, stirring occasionally, until the rhubarb is soft, about 10 minutes.

Filling perogies.
ROLF HICKER PHOTOGRAPHY

Potato Salad

Salad

8 to 12 potatoes, preferably Yukon Gold variety

12 eggs

1½ large English cucumbers,
seeded and chopped

2 cups (500 mL) chopped celery

1 Spanish onion, diced

3 bunches green onions, chopped

2 red bell peppers, cored and minced

2 green bell peppers, cored and minced

Dressing

1 cup (250 mL) mayonnaise,
preferably Miracle Whip

1 cup (250 mL) sour cream

1½ to 2 Tbsp (22.5 to 30 mL) yellow
mustard, preferably French's

1 tsp (5 mL) garlic powder (not garlic salt)

3 to 4 Tbsp (45 to 60 mL) white vinegar

3 or 4 sprigs fresh dill, finely chopped

Fresh parsley, finely chopped, to taste

Salt and pepper, to taste

Curry powder or red chili flakes (optional)

One hundred and forty-three years old, the Saanich Fair on Vancouver Island is the longest continuously running agriculture fair in Western Canada. As with all fairs, it showcases portly pigs, jumping horses, spitting llamas, pies, cakes, and preserves along with knitting, quilting, needlework, and highland dancing. It is still quite rural in its approach and attending takes me back to my roots so I always love going. I think the whole island turns out for the event.

I once won first prize at the Saanich Fair for this potato salad. The measurements for the vegetables can be suited to your taste. I like mine with lots of chopped vegetables.

Boil the potatoes whole, leaving the skins on. (I use Yukon Gold potatoes because they keep their shape and don't boil to mush.) When they are cool, remove the skins, cut into bite-sized chunks, and add to a large bowl. Store in the refrigerator until thoroughly chilled.

Hard-boil the eggs. When they are cool enough to handle, remove the shells, and then store in the refrigerator until chilled.

Dice the chilled eggs and chop the vegetables, and then add to the potatoes. Set aside while you make the dressing.

Add the ingredients for the dressing to a medium-sized bowl and stir. Adjust the amount of vinegar, spices, and mustard to your taste. (You can also add in curry powder or red chili flakes.) Fold the dressing into the salad mixture and mix gently. Cover and set in the refrigerator until serving.

Serves 8 to 12 people.

Christmas Salad

1 cup (250 mL) boiling water

1 3 oz package (100mL) lime JELL-O

½ cup (125 mL) crushed pineapple, drained

4 green onions, thinly sliced

½ cup (125 mL) grated carrots

½ cup (125 mL) diced celery

1 Red Delicious apple, cored
and cut into small pieces

Red and green diced maraschino cherries
(optional, for a festive appearance)

1 cup (250 mL) cottage cheese

½ cup (125 mL) mayonnaise,
preferably Miracle Whip

½ cup (125 mL) sour cream

This salad is very festive and signals Christmas for us. I sometimes also make it when I have family visiting from out of town and I want to dress up a meal.

Add the boiling water to a medium-sized bowl, and then add the JELL-O powder, stirring until the crystals are dissolved, about 2 minutes. Set the mixture aside and let cool to room temperature.

In another bowl, combine the pineapple, green onion, carrot, celery, apple, and cherries (if using), and gently blend together. In another bowl, mix together the cottage cheese, mayonnaise, and sour cream, and then fold it into the fruit and vegetable mixture.

Pour the cooled gelatin overtop and stir until blended. Transfer to a festive-shaped mold and refrigerate overnight.

Unmold the salad just before serving. If the salad does not come out of the mold right away, place the bottom of the mold in a pan of hot water for no more than 15 seconds.

Makes 12 servings.

Turkey Stuffing

1 lb (500 g) ground pork sausage meat
2 stalks of celery
2 large cooking onions
1 apple
Fresh parsley, finely chopped, to taste
2 tsp (10 mL) poultry seasoning
2 tsp (10 mL) dried sage
1 tsp (5 mL) salt
1 loaf dry white bread, cubed

I make this stuffing for our Christmas turkey. It is a recipe that I have experimented with over the years. It's not quite like my mother's. She didn't put celery in hers although we grew a lot of celery in the garden. You may want to change the spices to suit your taste; I do occasionally. This recipe is not set in stone.

Cook the pork sausage meat in a frying pan with a small bit of oil until it is cooked through, then let it cool just enough to handle (you want the stuffing to be warm when you put it in the turkey).

In a food processor, chop the celery, onions, and apple. Add this mixture to a large bowl, and then add the parsley and other seasonings. Stir in the cooked meat and bread cubes.

Stuff the turkey loosely, and truss the bird to keep the stuffing from falling out of the cavity. (Put any leftover stuffing in a greased, covered ovenproof dish and cook it in the oven for the last hour you are cooking the turkey.)

Note: It is important to follow government food safety practices when cooking a stuffed turkey. The center of the stuffing inside the turkey cavity should reach at least 165°F (74°C) before serving.

Makes enough stuffing for one average-sized turkey.

Raw Cranberry Compote

4 cups (1 L) fresh or frozen
cranberries, chopped

1 great big Red Delicious apple, diced

Zest of 1 orange

Zest of 1 lemon

½ cup (125 mL) sugar (or more,
if you like it sweeter)

What I like about this compote is that it tastes clean, cool, and fresh. I usually serve it with turkey but you can also put the compote in cooked tart shells and decorate them with a swirl of whipped cream if you like.

Chop the cranberries in a food processor. Dice the apple by hand. Wash the orange and lemon with hot, soapy water, and then dry them before zesting. (Be sure not to scrape the bitter white pith.)

Mix the chopped cranberries, diced apple, and zest in a bowl. Pour the sugar overtop, stir, and let stand until serving.

Makes 10 servings.

Bubbat

2 cups (500 mL) flour
2 tsp (10 mL) baking powder
Salt, to taste
2 Tbsp (30 mL) unsalted butter
12 prunes, diced
½ cup (125 mL) diced dried apricots
½ cup (125 mL) raisins
3 eggs, beaten
1 cup (250 mL) table cream
Gravy, for serving

This recipe comes from my Mennonite background. There are different types of Bubbat; some are made with yeast and others with sugar and whipping cream, to create something more cake-like. My recipe for Bubbat is one you can use as a side dish with a pork roast or as a nice addition to a delicious roast goose or duck.

Preheat the oven to 375°F (180°C) and grease an 8-inch (20-cm) square cake pan or glass baking dish.

Mix together the dry ingredients, and then cut in the butter. Add the fruit and mix with your fingers to coat the fruit evenly with the flour, which will keep it from sinking to the bottom of the pan during baking.

Add the eggs and enough cream to make a creamy batter. Your dough should be soft and somewhat difficult to stir with a spoon.

Pour the dough into the prepared pan or dish and bake for about 45 minutes, or until a cake tester comes out clean.

Cut the Bubbat into squares and ladle a generous spoonful of gravy overtop when serving.

Makes 8 servings.

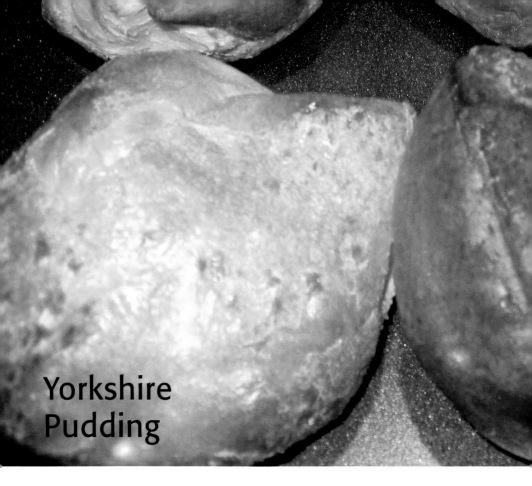

Yorkshire Pudding

3 eggs
1 cup (250 mL) milk
¼ tsp (1 mL) salt
1 cup (250 mL) all-purpose flour
Beef drippings from your roast
(or substitute lard or Crisco)

This side dish is very nice served with a roast beef dinner. You can make individual puddings in a muffin tin, or you can use a cast-iron frying pan, as I do, to make one very large pudding that is quite impressive.

Preheat the oven to 450°F (240°C). Beat the eggs with a wire whisk until they are frothy. Add the milk, flour, and salt and continue beating until well mixed. Set the batter aside to rest for about 30 minutes.

Add a small bit of fat to your muffin tin or frying pan and put in the oven. Remove when the fat is smoking hot, about 5 minutes.

Add the Yorkshire pudding batter and return to the oven. Cook for 15 to 20 minutes and then reduce the heat to 350°F (180°C). Continue baking for another 10 to 15 minutes. Turn on the oven light so you can see how the pudding is doing. You should see a lovely, puffy, golden-brown work of art when it's done. Don't open your oven too early or the Yorkshire pudding will fall.

Serve immediately with a generous ladleful of roast beef gravy poured overtop.

Makes 1 dozen.

Pamela Anderson holding her Great-Auntie Vie's honey mustard in one hand and pickles in the other.
WITH PERMISSION OF PAMELA ANDERSON. PHOTO COURTESY OF CAROL ANDERSON

Auntie Vie's Prize-Winning Honey Mustard

4 cups (1 L) dry mustard powder
3 cups (750 mL) all-purpose flour
2 to 2¼ cups (500 to 560 mL) honey
1½ cups (375 mL) sugar
3 ¾ cups (935 mL) white vinegar

This recipe has a sweet taste of honey laced throughout the mustard. It is thick enough to spread on bread and is a nice condiment for meats. I have won several awards for this mustard and my neighbor tells me she eats it by the spoonful right out of the jar.

Assemble canning jars, rings, lids, and a wide-mouth canning funnel, plus glass or stainless-steel bowls, pots, and spoons (uncoated metal will not only leave an unpleasant aftertaste in the mustard but it is also toxic).

Follow standard government health and safety procedures for sterilizing your jars and lids. Once the jars have been sterilized, turn them upside down on a clean rack to dry; you want them completely dry before you fill them because even the tiniest bit of water will ruin the mustard.

In a large mixing bowl, mix together the mustard powder, flour, honey, and sugar.

One cup at a time, stir in the vinegar. You want to add enough vinegar to make a creamy paste, but still thick enough to spread with a butter knife. Taste for sweetness and add more honey if needed. It will take a few days for the ingredients to blend into each other, so the mustard might taste a little less sweet the day you make it than it will two days later.

Spoon the mustard into the sterilized jars using the wide-mouth funnel. Wipe off any mustard from the tops of the jars with dry paper towels.

When the jars are filled, cap them with the sterilized lids and secure them with the rings that came with the jars. You will not get a vacuum seal so you must store the mustard in the refrigerator.

Let the mustard rest for a few days before you open your first jar. (Always store the mustard with the lid on, otherwise it will dry out and harden.)

Makes 9 half-pint (236 mL) jars.

COURTESY OF EILEEN ZAPSHALA

Refrigerator Dill Pickles

8 fresh, firm baby pickling cucumbers

3 stalks fresh dillweed

2 to 3 tiny red dried chili peppers, like serranos

3 garlic cloves, peeled

Brine

3 cups (750 mL) water,
preferably soft or distilled

1 cup (250 mL) white pickling vinegar

1 Tbsp (15 mL) pickling salt

¼ tsp (1 mm) food-grade alum

I have won many awards for these pickles. If you live in an area with hard water, use distilled water because hard water will reduce the acidity level, which can cause the growth of unwanted bacteria in the pickles. It's also important to use pickling vinegar because it has a higher acidity level than ordinary white vinegar. Finally, don't use table salt because it will darken the pickles and make them mushy (and you will be able to taste the iodine in the salt).

It's a little difficult to tell you how much this recipe makes. It really depends on how many jars of pickles you want. Just keep filling the jars and adding the brine until you have what you want.

Assemble proper quart-size (1 L) canning jars, rings, and new lids, making sure there are no nicks, chips, or cracks on any part of the jars.

Wash the cucumbers and nip off the top stems, being careful not cut into the cucumbers themselves. The stem contains an enzyme that can soften the pickles.

Pack the cucumbers into a large pan or set them in the sink surrounded by lots of ice. Let them chill for 1 to 2 hours, which will help keep the cucumbers crisp.

Follow standard government health and safety procedures for sterilizing the jars, lids, and rings. After sterilizing them, don't let them sit for long; you want to use them almost immediately while they are still hot.

Into each sterilized jar, place 3 long stalks of dill. I curl them up to get them in the jar. Add 2 to 3 chili peppers and 3 cloves peeled garlic. Add the cucumbers, packing them in vertically. Set aside while you prepare the brine.

Use only stainless steel or glass pots, bowls, and utensils when making the brine since uncoated metals are toxic when mixed with acids like vinegar.

For every 3 cups (750 mL) water you put in the pot you're using to make the brine, add 1 cup (250 mL) pickling vinegar, 1 tablespoon (15 mL) pickling salt, and ¼ teaspoon (1 mL) alum. Rather that doubling or tripling up on the measurements, I repeat this process each time until the pot is full. (This may seem odd but I find that it is easy to get distracted and lose track of measuring.)

Cook the brine on medium-high heat until just before the boiling point.

Pour the hot brine into the packed jars, filling them all the way up to the top so it covers the pickles completely.

Run a knife or spatula through the pickles to release any air bubbles. If there is any brine on the rims of the jars, wipe it off with a clean paper towel. Put the sterilized lids on the jars and screw on the rings. Turn the jars upside down and leave them on the counter for 24 hours to cool.

The next day, set the jars upright, rinse them off under the tap, and tighten the rings if any are loose. Do not overtighten because you can break the seal. You can tell a jar is sealed if the center of the lid is lower than the sides and it does not move up and down when you press on it.

Store the sealed jars in the refrigerator and let sit for about five weeks before you open them. If any of the jars have failed to seal, put them in the refrigerator anyway and eat those ones first.

As these pickles are not processed in a hot-water bath, it is important to store them in the refrigerator, which also helps to keep them crisp and crunchy. Sometimes the garlic turns a bit blue but unless there are other signs of spoilage they are safe to eat. Garlic contains sulfur compounds and will react to minute traces of copper in the water or vinegar.

Makes a 1-quart (1 L) jar. Multiply amount of ingredients accordingly to make additional jars.

Auntie Vie in the Bengal Room of the Fairmont Empress Hotel.
ROLF HICKER PHOTOGRAPHY

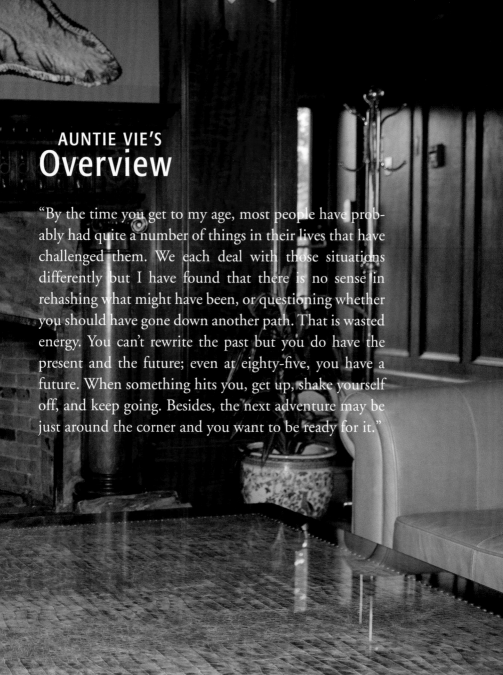

AUNTIE VIE'S
Overview

"By the time you get to my age, most people have probably had quite a number of things in their lives that have
challenged them. We each deal with those situations
differently but I have found that there is no sense in
rehashing what might have been, or questioning whether
you should have gone down another path. That is wasted
energy. You can't rewrite the past but you do have the
present and the future; even at eighty-five, you have a
future. When something hits you, get up, shake yourself
off, and keep going. Besides, the next adventure may be
just around the corner and you want to be ready for it."

Acknowledgments

I can't even begin to describe how much fun it has been to work with Auntie Vie. Her enthusiasm and patience knew no bounds. She opened her heart and shared her life story with me, and she taught me a lot about cooking and about fashion. She provided useful hints on aging gracefully and made me laugh. It has been the most inspirational and deliciously delightful book I have ever worked on.

A very special thank-you goes to Rolf Hicker, a photographer with extraordinary talent. He and his wife came to stay with my husband and me while their newborn baby was in the neonatal intensive care unit of our local hospital. Worried about his baby and exhausted from lack of sleep, he nonetheless gave unselfishly of his time to spend a week photographing Auntie Vie and following her around to various celebrity events. Rolf is well known nationally and internationally for his work as a nature, travel, and wildlife photographer and as a filmmaker, and his website is one of the most popular travel websites on the Internet; check it out at www.hickerphoto.com.

I would also like to thank Carol Anderson for sharing her insights about her aunt with me. Like her mother, Auntie Vie's sister Rose, Carol is a beautiful and vivacious lady who is devoted to her family. I would also like to thank Pamela Anderson, for taking time out of a very busy schedule to share her lovely thoughts about her great-auntie with us. (Pamela, I don't think your auntie is finished with her block parties just yet.)

/A\ Vancouver Island has been a big supporter of Auntie Vie. They have showcased her fashion, spotlighted her charm and her wit, eaten her pickles, and dined on her dishes—wait until you try her Bailey's Irish Cream Coconut Bread Pudding—and shared their impressions with the viewing public. They introduced us to a remarkable woman and treated Auntie Vie with respect and integrity; Auntie Vie has a very special place in her heart for Adam Sawatsky and the team at /A\ News. I would like to thank Rob Anderson, the manager of Afternoon Tea at the Fairmont Empress, for his graciousness in letting Rolf and me film Auntie Vie while she was judging the Great Poutine Cookoff between executive chefs Takashi Ito of the Fairmont Empress and Brad Horen of the Inn at Laurel Point in Victoria, British Columbia.

I would also like to thank publisher Ruth Linka and her team at TouchWood Editions for their support and help. They are the people who quietly toil behind the scenes to bring a book like this one to fruition, and I couldn't ask to work with a better group.

Lastly, I offer a debt of gratitude to all of her family members for sharing a small piece of Auntie Vie with us. I know she loves you all; you mean the world to her.

Cathy Converse is the author of *Following the Curve of Time* and *Mainstays: Women Who Shaped BC*, the co-author of *The Remarkable World of Frances Barkley*, and the co-editor of *In Her Own Right: Selected Essays on the History of Women in BC*. She is a founder of the Camosun College Women's Studies curriculum and ancillary programs, and a former department chair and instructor. Cathy is also Auntie Vie's neighbor.